A Catholic Handbook for Engaged and Newly Married Couples

Front Cover: *"The Flight into Egypt,"* 17th Century, by Bartolome Esteban Murillo. © Copyright The Detroit Institute of Arts, Gift of Mr. and Mrs. K. T. Keller, Mr. and Mrs. Leslie H. Green and Mr. and Mrs. Robert N. Green.

A Catholic Handbook for Engaged and Newly Married Couples

by
Frederick W. Marks, Ph.D.

Faith Publishing Co.
P.O. Box 237
Milford, OH 45150

NIHIL OBSTAT: Rev. Jonathan Morse
June 1, 1994
Stamford, Connecticut
Censor

IMPRIMATUR: ✠ Most Rev. Basil H. Losten
Bishop of Stamford
June 2, 1994

NIHIL OBSTAT: The Reverend Richard W. Ferris, STL
Delegated Censor

IMPRIMATUR: ✠ Thomas V. Daily, D.D.
Bishop of Brooklyn
Brooklyn, NY
June 2, 1994

The *nihil obstat* and/or *imprimatur* are official declarations that a book or pamphlet is free of doctrinal or moral error. No implication is contained therein that those who have granted the *nihil obstat* and *imprimatur* agree with the contents, opinions or statements expressed.

The Marks family has affiliation with both the Byzantine Ukrainian and Roman rites of the Catholic Church; hence the dual *imprimatur.*

Published by: FAITH PUBLISHING COMPANY
P.O. BOX 237
MILFORD, OHIO 45150

Additional copies of this book may be acquired by contacting:

For bookstores: Faith Publishing Company
P.O. Box 237
Milford, Ohio 45150
1-800-576-6477

For individuals: The Riehle Foundation
P.O. Box 7
Milford, Ohio 45150
1-513-576-0032

TO MARY ANNE

Table of Contents

Publisher's Preface

A Catholic Handbook for Engaged and Newly Married Couples fills a void. This book addresses virtually every facet of engagement and married life which people who are approaching and living the Sacrament of Matrimony need to know.

Frederick W. Marks, Ph.D., offers us a chance to look at the standards our Church has consistently taught as valuable to maintain when preparing for and living the marriage commitment. He not only details what is expected of married couples by the Church, but he also explains the critical *why.*

A particular benefit of this book is the appendix. It should not be overlooked. Dr. Marks provides a fascinating resource section, including a comprehensive questionnaire for engaged couples to use. It is intended to bring about discussion, prior to the wedding day, of potential difficulties which couples might need to assess. It can also be used later in married life as a basis for examining where a couple is in their relationship, how they are progressing toward their goals, and simply keeping the lines of communication open.

Modern society has effectively eliminated respect for the holy state of matrimony. The Catholic Church has always spoken clearly about Her expectations for those who choose this beautiful vocation, but Her voice is muffled by the dissent of people who view marriage as divorced from the spiritual aspect of our nature. They see marriage through the eyes of secular humanism. Our culture is experiencing the frightful repercussions which are the result of the lack of moral values which has become the norm.

The feminist movement, the gay rights movement, and various other liberal movements, most of which can accurately be labeled "pro-choice," have condemned the vocation of marriage as an obsolete remnant of less sophisticated times. Cohabitation without benefit of marriage (fornication) has become common. Illegitimate births are at an all-time high. Artificial contraception is promoted as an essential good. Abortion is the scourge of our once great land. Homosexuality and every possible perversion are glamourized and promoted as viable options—even in our schools.

Crime, drug abuse, and every form of addiction are rampant. Poverty has become multi-generational. Personal responsibility and ethical behavior are rejected as passé. Innocent, God-fearing people are suffering. The family, as the basic societal unit, has been stifled.

Child-rearing has given way to freedom for children, where the young have the opportunity and encouragement (even from teachers) to reject the morals of their parents. In effect, they are being taught (via television, rock music, and attitudes encouraged in many classrooms) to ignore and disrespect their parents.

Parents often give up or give in. For the sake of keeping "peace" in their homes, they sacrifice their right to discipline their children, and, instead, they become their children's buddies. The tails now wag the dogs.

The calling of married Christians has not changed. Our holy Church and Her teachings have not changed. What was good in the past worked: following the laws set forth by God in Sacred Scripture and interpreted in a consistently moral fashion throughout Church Tradition for almost 2,000 years resulted in progress for humanity as never before witnessed on earth.

But, we are now past the crossroads. Society is too far down the wrong path. In our country, and even in our holy Church, many have laid aside the truths of the past, clinging instead to a sense of liberation from light and goodness, from responsibility, from truth, and, ultimately, from God. We need to return to the crossroads, realize we have taken a wrong turn, and proceed down the long, narrow path of righteousness. The best place to begin the journey is in the domestic Church—the home.

It is never too late to make changes in our lives for the better. During the special time of engagement and the early years of marriage, when the thrill of new love and romance makes all wonderful things seem possible, outlooks are most optimistic. This is an excellent time for couples to forge personal bonds of commitment, not only to themselves, but as witnesses to the world of the beauty that God created for us to enjoy if we do His will. They can truly offer a great gift to God—and humanity—simply by living the way He intends. And God will reward the gracious acceptance of His will. He cannot and will not be outdone in generosity!

*   *   *   *   *

Frederick W. Marks is a research historian and essayist with degrees from Holy Cross College and the University of Michigan. The author of four previous books and numerous articles published both at home and abroad, he has taught courses on the fundamentals of the Catholic faith at the university level, as well as at his local parish. He and his wife, Sylvia, have been happily married for twenty-seven years, and they live with their daughter, Mary Anne, in Forest Hills, New York.

—Faith Publishing Company

Acknowledgments

I should like to thank the following persons for taking the time to read rough drafts of this handbook and for offering valuable suggestions: Father Kenneth Baker, S.J.; Father Avery Dulles, S.J.; Reverend Peter M. J. Stravinskas; Reverend Robert D. Smith, religious columnist for *The Wanderer;* Father James Torrens, S.J., of *America* magazine; Reverend John McCloskey III, chaplain of Mercer House, Princeton; Drs. Raúl and Liliana Alessandri, along with Dave and Phyllis Burns, pre-Cana instructors in the New York Archdiocese; Anne Carroll, Catholic educator and author; Patricia Pucetti; Dr. Michael Karol; Mary Frances Lester; John Metzler; Bill and Frances Reck, my publishers; Laurie Balbach-Taylor, my editor; and last, but not least, my wife, Sylvia, sweetheart and best friend for over twenty-five years, who contributed in every way imaginable.

Foreword

It is not easy to find authentically Catholic books and pamphlets to help engaged and newly married couples. Unfortunately, many of them are defective, either because they reject important aspects of Catholic teaching on marriage and family life, or because they simply omit things the authors do not agree with, such as the immorality of artificial contraception. There are no such problems with Dr. Frederick Marks' brief Catholic handbook.

This handbook is outstanding both for its practicality and for its fidelity to the Catholic faith. It is practical because it offers good suggestions on most aspects of married life, such as the wedding, the honeymoon, the relationship between husband and wife, in-laws, finances, raising children, sexual relations, practicing the faith, and developing a spiritual life of personal relations with God.

The handbook is also thoroughly Catholic. It offers excellent advice on how to live the Catholic faith as a married man or woman. There is no waffling here, no dissent, no ambiguity. The author spells out clearly what the Catholic Church expects of married people in the areas of married life, sexuality, and family life.

Of course, there is no such thing as a "quick fix" or an easy solution to the difficulties to be faced by any man and woman who commit themselves to each other for life. It is not easy for any two people to live together day in and day out without some disagreement and friction. But

Dr. Marks gives engaged and newly married couples some advance warnings on what to expect, and, even more importantly, he offers some sage advice on how to deal with problems—advice which is based on his own experience and on the accumulated wisdom of the Catholic Church.

So if you are looking for some help to make your Catholic marriage the best it can possibly be, in my opinion, you will be amply rewarded by a careful reading and reflection on this handbook and by having a frank discussion of it with your spouse.

—Fr. Kenneth Baker, S.J.

Part 1
Introduction to Matrimony

Marriage is like a fine wine; it improves with age and appreciates in value. Torrents of worries and difficulties are incapable of drowning true love because people who sacrifice themselves generously are brought closer together in the long run...

Blessed Josemaría Escrivá de Balaguer

Never be cynical about love, for in the face of all aridity and disenchantment, it is as perennial as the grass...

Max Ehrmann

There is nothing in the world—no possible success, military or political, which is worth weighing in the balance for one moment against the happiness that comes to those fortunate enough to make a real love match—a match in which lover and sweetheart will never be lost in husband and wife. I know what I am writing about, for I am just as much devoted to Mrs. Roosevelt now as ever I was...

Theodore Roosevelt
President of the United States (1901-1909)
at the age of forty

WHAT DO YOU THINK OF MARRIAGE?

Marriage has been variously described as a great work, a great adventure, a great responsibility, and a great joy. Needless to say, it is all of these, not to mention a great disappointment to those who approach it irreverently or

1

ill prepared. But above all, marriage is a great vocation, full of grace for those who give to it all that they are and possess. Scripture tells us that Jesus blessed the wedding feast at Cana with a sudden burst of spiritual energy, nothing less than His first public miracle. Surely, He must have thought the occasion a worthy one.[1]

My parents used to say that although their life together was not always smooth sailing—they had their share of arguments—it was nonetheless worth it. And so it was. Have you ever known anyone to be unhappy who was happily married? Many, on the other hand, with successful careers and a high standard of living, feel emotionally devastated because they are insecure at home or because their marriage has crashed. The right partner will bring out the best in you, soothing your heart when it aches and tapping hidden strengths—in short, helping you to make of the "lumber of your life not a tavern, but a temple." You, in turn, will do the same for your better half, just as the two of you, working together, will afford solace and comfort to friends and neighbors by the warmth of your hospitality.

The other side of the coin is that the same spouse who soothes will also irritate, tempting you at times to commit everything short of hari-kari. Marriage multiplies responsibilities and puts one to the test in unforeseen ways. If, based on what you are able to observe, you are a bit apprehensive because you sense a stiff challenge ahead, you are right. With all of its rewards, matrimony makes demands. Like life itself, it requires that we possess the desire and the will to grow as people. Those, therefore, who may be looking, first and foremost, for what they can get out of it are in for a big disappointment because

---

1. Pope John Paul II, in his *Letter to Families* for 1994, the "Year of the Family," calls marriage "a true vocation" as well as "a great mystery" (quoting Paul). See sections 18 and 19.

conjugal love means giving rather than getting. It means having to say one is sorry and saying it often. Instead of using your spouse for your own ends, you will find yourself sacrificing for the good of the marriage. Time and again, you and your partner will extend yourselves to the absolute limit because love that is true knows no bounds, and true love is the only kind that lasts.

A great saint by the name of Catherine of Siena once had a vision that God was offering her many crosses, some small, others large. Anxious to please, she selected the heaviest. "No," said the Lord, "that one is not for you. It is reserved for married couples." Catherine's insight may be a trifle mischievous, but it serves as a useful corrective to the prevailing notion that it is somehow easier to be married than to lead a chaste single life. Where is the evidence for such an assumption? Whatever our state in life, whether we are single, married, or bound by religious vows, there will be trials. The thing to bear in mind is that God has promised each and every one of us all the means necessary to carry on, and to carry on beautifully, provided we do what we can to cooperate. And that, of course, is where pre-Cana comes in. Before athletes enter competition, they prepare. Before soldiers go into battle, they train. And the same holds true of marriage. As in sport and combat, there is no substitute for preparation. Marriage handbooks may not simulate actual "field" conditions, but in many ways they can come close, and it will be the aim of the following pages to come as close as possible.

Even if there were no trend afoot to treat matrimony lightly and to discount the whole idea of life-long fidelity, there would still be a need to prepare for marriage, just as one prepares for any signal event in life. Priestly vocations are brought to fruition by years of seminary training. Ambitious parents aiming at a prestigious Ivy League education for their youngster go out of their way to enroll the child in the right nursery school. A lengthy apprenticeship is necessary to become a full-fledged plumber or electrician. Many newlyweds anticipate parenthood by attending a series of childbirth courses. Yet ironically, in one of the most vital commitments of all, marriage itself, the only courses seem to appear after the fact: "Parenting Without a Partner," "Handling Your Divorce," or "Making It in the Post-Marriage Singles World."

Curiously enough, the Catholic Church is one of the few institutions in the world that requires some type of formal instruction before marriage, and this is due, in large part, to its insistence on the sacramental and binding nature of the union.

As Catholics, we reject categorically the idea of divorce and remarriage, believing that no marriage, however ill-advised or troubled, is ever beyond redemption. When we pledge our loyalty "for better or worse," "in sickness and in health," what we are saying in effect is that nothing, absolutely nothing, can ever invalidate our commitment: not cancer, not paralysis, not childlessness, not alcoholism, not even infidelity. Separation may be warranted in extreme cases, but never divorce and remarriage. This is one of the cardinal tenets of Catholic teaching, firmly in place for nearly two thousand years, and it comes directly from Christ, as well as St. Paul.[2] Jesus restored marriage to its original ideal after it had been debased by polygamy, divorce, and adultery.

We are all aware that ecclesiastical authorities have been known, on occasion, to grant a declaration of nullity (commonly known as an "annulment"), stating that, in the absence of certain preconditions, a marriage never took place (in the sense that the contract between consenting parties that is required for marriage was never

---

2. See appendix B.

valid to begin with.)[3] Critics are quick to suggest that annulment is merely divorce, Catholic style. But this is not so. Abuses there have been, particularly in the United States in recent years owing to the human side of the Church, and such abuses may have undermined the Church's credibility. But we should not be put off. Clerical compromisers are a well-known breed in Church history, leaders who capitulated to the "powers that be" either out of weakness or genuine pastoral concern. What is heartening is that the Church is still the Church. It is still teaching essentially what it taught two millennia ago. Christ's vicar on earth has been totally consistent over the years in holding that once a valid union is contracted, it is indissoluble—that is, unbreakable. Prominent figures such as Bishop John Fisher and Sir Thomas More of England gave their very lives in defense of this principle which remains to this day one of the most precious jewels in the crown of our faith.

Apart from the fact that divorce has been linked with the likelihood of early death from strokes, hypertension, respiratory and intestinal cancer; apart, too, from the fact that children from broken homes are more likely to do poorly in school, abuse drugs, break the law, and attempt suicide, nothing could be more positive or more healthy than the Catholic stand on indissolubility.[4] And the reason is simple. Only if one is committed to giving one's all, only when we are shielded from the temptation to look for a way out when caught in the eye of the storm, does marriage come into its own. Conversely, the

---

3. See appendix C.
4. Philip Yancy, "God is Good for You," *Catholic Digest* (February 1992), p. 2. Judges have required applicants for divorce to take upward of four hours of courses to familiarize themselves with the horrendous ills visited on the children of divorced parents (*New York Times*, 23 January 1992, p. C8).

moment one accepts the possibility of divorce and remarriage, even for serious reasons, one is sanctioning divorce
on demand, for whose reasons are not serious? And with
what result? All marriages, even sound ones, wind up
on shaky ground.

Given today's moral climate with its stress on situation
ethics, married couples are an endangered species. The
fact that half of them choose to separate is a pretty sure
sign that many, if not most, among the remainder, must
be struggling just to keep up appearances. One might
add, on the basis of statistics, that the rate of failure for
those who remarry is staggeringly high, higher even than
the 50 percent associated with first marriages. Further-
more, according to a recent survey conducted by
researchers at the University of Virginia, 72 percent of all
divorcées are convinced, within two years of marital
breakup, that their divorce was a mistake.[5]

Naturally, the more serious we are about marriage, the
more anxious we will be to prepare, especially if we
believe there can be no turning back. It is an interesting
commentary on today's society that jurors selected in
some places for federal trial duty are likely to receive a
more thorough cross-examination than many young people contemplating marriage. The judge will try to ascertain if they have any emotional blocks, prejudices, or
compromising relationships, any "chips on the shoul-
der," so to speak, that could prove damaging. They will
be quizzed on their understanding of the essentials of the
law and asked if, once in deliberation, they expect to
have enough gumption to stick to their opinion even if
they find themselves a minority of one. Attorneys on both
sides will also want to know if potential jurors are humble enough to reassess their position should they be con-

---

5. *National Catholic Register,* 24 May 1992, p. 5 (the percentage for
   men was also high: 61 percent).

vinced by fellow jurors, in the heat of argument, that they are wrong. Humility...courage...understanding... emotional fitness—these are the very same traits required for a successful marriage.

No couple wants to have their relationship examined with a fine tooth comb and to have questions tossed at them once they have settled on a definite course of action. But those who submit cheerfully can rest assured that if their intentions are pleasing in God's sight, nothing on the face of the earth is going to thwart them. If, on the other hand, there are underlying problems, now is the time to face them. If you are headed for trouble, now is the time to reconsider. If, on the other hand, you are on the right track, your chance for a smooth and happy adjustment will be greatly enhanced by going into marriage with both eyes open. Love need not be blind. The fewer surprises the better.

Part 2

Preparation

Presumably, by the time you are engaged, you have dated a number of different individuals. Not that this is essential, but ask yourself if you would want to buy the first house shown to you by a real estate broker. It is much the same in the choice of a husband or wife. A good way to become aware of differences is to get to know people from varied backgrounds. Obviously, the more you have in common with your spouse in the way of goals and ideals, hobbies and interests, the better the prospect for lasting happiness.

It goes without saying, too, that you have chosen each other for the right reasons and that you enjoyed one another's company for a reasonable period of time prior to engagement. Hopefully, by the time you became serious, you were able to observe how your partner handles stress in various forms. How do you relate to one another's friends and relatives? How do you react to disappointments and setbacks? Infatuation based on the glamour of a few dates or on sheer physical attraction is bound to fade, and if you are sensible, you are not marrying simply to please your parents or to gain financial security. Neither are you undertaking a life-long commitment merely to raise your social status or to satisfy some biological urge. Such motives will not suffice to carry you through life.

Let us assume, in addition, that you have considered a religious vocation, along with a chaste single life, as alternatives to marriage, for only if you have decided, after prayerful reflection, that marriage is the way God is calling you and your fiancée to carry out your mission in life (which is to know Him, to love Him, and to serve Him) should you proceed with your wedding plans.

To go a step further, how do you feel about the possibility of having children? If you are not willing to accept them as a gift from God or are presently unable to support a family financially, it would be wise to postpone your wedding until such time as things change.

How noble it is to share with God in the conception of immortal life and to lead young souls along the road to sanctity! Procreation may not be the only end of marriage. But it is a primary end, central to the plan of creation. One might almost call it a "mission" since each child is not only a gift bestowed on the family by God but also a great gift of the family *to* God. In addition, children contribute immeasurably to the growth of such traits as sensitivity, patience, wisdom, endurance, and holiness in their parents.

Marriage as a vocation aims at nothing less than the rearing of saints who will provide the "leaven" that our world so desperately needs and who will ultimately take their place beside their Maker in Heaven. Granted, parents cannot guarantee the salvation of their children. But neither is this required of them. All God asks is that they do their part. The rest is up to Him, in conjunction with the children themselves, and we can rest assured that He will hold up His end of the bargain. Francis Thompson's "Hound of Heaven" never rests! So there is every reason to rejoice and be glad.

As for couples who are not blessed with offspring, we can be sure that they are richly compensated in other ways. God is all loving and all good. More on this later.

And what if you are planning to marry a non-Catholic? The closer your partner comes to sharing your moral and religious values, the happier and more stable your union is going to be, as religion is bound to affect the way a person thinks and behaves. In spite of the optimism of those who assume that conjugal affection will bridge all gaps, religious differences constitute a definite basis for conflict, especially in regard to having children and providing for their education. To their credit, both parties may be strong and morally upright. Both may hope to win over the other in the long run. Ironically, the finer and more zealous the parties to such a match, the greater the likelihood of tension. Non-Catholics have as much of a right to want their children molded along cherished lines of thought and belief as Catholics. This is an area, therefore, that needs to be well thought out and thoroughly discussed before marriage so that resolutions can be made as to how and when the family will pray together as a unit and how the children will be encouraged (not merely *permitted,* but *encouraged*) to grow in the practice of their faith.

For many years the Church forbade Catholics to marry persons of another religion, and exceptions were made only for grave reasons. Why? Because experience indicates that "mixed" marriages (and this includes marriage to a luke-warm Catholic, as well as to a non-Catholic) are generally a source of discord and unhappiness for the entire family. All too often, such marriages result in religious indifference or loss of faith on the part of the Catholic, as well as a home atmosphere detrimental to the religious formation of the children. Both parties should be aware of the risks so they are prepared to make up the difference in other ways. In particular, there must be a clear understanding that one's offspring are to be raised and educated in the faith. This is Church law, and, as such, it binds the conscience of the Catholic.

Finally, how do you feel about engagement itself? You should be elated. Anxiety about plans and arrangements is natural. There may even be some inner doubt about one's ability to "measure up," but you should be happy and relieved to be on your way.

Beyond this, engagement calls for a certain degree of vigilance and self-control. Now is the time to display the kind of fidelity that will be indispensable later on. Obviously, there should be no flirting with third parties or playing hard to get. Neither should one be taking physical liberties of the kind reserved for marriage.[6]

Even if prolonged kissing, petting, hugging, and necking of the type calculated to arouse sexual passion were not sinful, all of this would be risky because of where it is likely to lead. The marriage contract, to be valid, requires freedom of choice, and such freedom is automatically impaired by excessive sexual involvement. The moment one becomes involved on the physical level to the point where marriage becomes something that is "owed," rather than freely given, one forfeits an important element of choice. There must be no high-pressure salesman standing over you when you make the most critical decision of your life. Many an argument for divorce turns on the premise that a person did not really "will" marriage, but rather slipped into it or was pressured by force of circumstance.

So, in a word, if you are trying to guard your courtship and take the high road, keep it up. This is the prudent, as well as the correct, course if you are serious about the future.

It is easy to fall for the line that premarital sex, in the sense of "living together," helps couples find out whether or not they are compatible. Nothing could be

---

6. According to the newly published universal *Catechism of the Catholic Church* (1994), engaged couples "should reserve for marriage the expressions of affection that belong to married love" (section 2350).

farther from the truth. Sex outside of marriage can't come anywhere near simulating the conditions of marital union because the situations are radically different, with different responsibilities, different expectations, different commitments, and an entirely different psychological "feel." One's mate outside marriage is apt to appear more attractive (or less so) than he or she would actually be wearing a wedding band. Just as apples and oranges are similar in shape but not in taste, so too with licit and illicit sex. Sin is never a good place to discover the truth. Besides, it is rare that two people who love one another for the right reasons and who are compatible in other ways turn out to have serious physiological problems.

By one recent estimate, 40 percent of those who live together before marriage never make it to the altar, and of those who do, the divorce rate is significantly higher than it is for other couples. Fornicators are thus putting whatever children may be born of such a union at grave risk.[7] In other words, apart from the sanction upheld by every major religion, common sense alone would dictate the avoidance of an act which, in the view of psychologists, is likely to leave permanent scars. Once you have given yourself totally to another human being, it is doubtful that you will ever be able to do so again in quite the same way.

And what if you are already on the wrong road? It is never too late to turn back. With a sincere desire for God's forgiveness and a firm purpose of amendment, you can still receive the Sacrament of Matrimony worthily. Although fornication (the name given by the Bible to premarital sex) is a definite offense against God, as well as against the virtue and honor of one's betrothed, the Lord is unfailingly kind and compassionate. It is just that He expects three very definite things of us: contrition, con-

---

7. *Our Sunday Visitor,* 27 December 1992, p. 23. See also *New York Times,* 9 June 1989, p. A1; *National Catholic Register,* 7 May 1989, p. 5.

fession, and penance. In a word, if you have engaged in pre-marital intercourse or if you are living with your intended spouse, now is the time to stop, go to confession, and do whatever penance is prescribed by the priest. In this way, you will retain your freedom, and God will smile on you the way the father of the gospel story smiled on his prodigal son. Let the white of the bridal gown be a true symbol of virtue, the diamond a real token of lasting happiness. Be honest with yourselves, with society, and with your Maker.

No one would claim that chastity is an easy virtue to live. If it were, everyone would be living it. No, it can be diffi-cult, which is why long engagements are not usually recom-mended. Nevertheless, it is well within the range of the possible for those who are (a) convinced that this is what the Lord is asking of them, and (b) confident that, if they persist in prayer, their Heavenly Father will furnish them with grace sufficient to avoid places and situations that are likely to be occasions of sin. Did Jesus Himself not say, *"Ask and you shall receive. Seek and you shall find. Knock and the door shall be opened to you"* (*Matt.* 7:7)?

Such counsel may sound almost quaint at a time when we are bombarded on every side by advice of a different kind. But with the Lord's help, all things are possible, and if, for some reason, the kind of restraint to which we are referring seems out of reach, you have reason to be con-cerned, for if there is anything the married state demands it is self-possession. Without this, one is only leading oneself and one's fiancée down the primrose path.

Ours is an age in which the statistics on abortion, vene-real disease, teenage suicide, and divorce are sky high and rising.[8] At the same time, this very society which has

---

8. There is no nation in the world, not even Sweden, where the divorce rate is as high as it is in the United States (*Christian Science Monitor,* 26 January 1987, p. 21). According to *Our Sunday Visitor* (27 Decem-ber 1992, p. 23), "Divorce tripled since 1960, and illegitimacy soared fourfold, even though abortions tripled over the past 20 years."

proven such a failure when it comes to sexual adjustment, continues to palm off its trendy wisdom on millions of young people who crave a "modern" lifestyle.

Think about it. If there were a village somewhere in the world with a life expectancy of twenty-three and where four out of six infants died before reaching the age of five, would you want to adopt its diet and imitate its customs? If you believe it makes any sense in a culture such as ours to attempt to be "one of the crowd," then a Catholic marriage is not for you. If, on the other hand, you are open to a code of sexual conduct with a proven track record, one that is perfectly capable of serving the present age, then proceed. We cannot say that "everyone is doing it." But then you are not "everyone." Hopefully, you will have second thoughts before setting yourself up for a life of disillusionment which seems to be more and more the common lot.

ENGAGEMENT

Engagement is a time to draw closer to God, the source of all happiness, and if you are sensible, you will make this approach a joint venture. Why not arrange to receive the sacraments as a couple so as to pave the way for the kind of pattern you hope to establish later on? Perhaps, too, one or both of you will write a wedding prayer that can be recited down through the crowded years of your marriage, one that will evoke fond memories of a glorious day. Why not attend an extra weekday Mass? The Holy Eucharist is powerful. If you are fortunate enough to live or work in an area where celebration of the Liturgy is frequent, you may find that you can receive Communion before work, during lunch break, or on the way home. Accompany your preparation for marriage with daily sincere prayer for a partner whom you can freely and truly love; one you truly wish "to have and to hold, from this day forward, for better, for worse, for richer, for poorer,

in sickness and in health, until death do us part." Could
you squeeze in a Rosary while you ride a bus or wait in
line, or perhaps sign up for a weekend retreat?

Granted, engagement is also a time to make wedding
plans, to take stock of finances, and to think seriously
about what will be needed to maintain a household.
Generally speaking, you would be ill-advised to start out
under someone else's roof, well-intentioned as that someone else might be. Nor would it be advisable to enter marriage under a heavy load of financial obligation. A fair
number of divorce cases involve people who are head-
over-heels in debt. When one of my wife's college friends
suddenly decided to postpone her marriage, originally
scheduled immediately after graduation, everyone was
shocked, wondering if the courtship had soured. They
were even more astounded when she announced that
because she and her fiancé could not afford children, they
were not tying the knot until they could; hence the post-
ponement. So far as we know, this couple is still happily
married!

When I was growing up, breadwinners could usually
count on earning a "living wage," enabling one or the
other parent, normally the wife, to stay home with the
children. Since this is no longer the rule and since such
expedients as artificial birth control, sterilization, and
abortion are morally impermissible, couples are wise to
build some kind of a financial base before becoming
engaged. In some cases, this could mean living with one's
parents for an interval while holding down a full-time job,
winning promotion, and saving every penny. In others, it
might be a matter of living alone and saving less, but
delaying engagement or marriage still further until the
basic elements of financial security are in place. If, in
addition, there is a mutual willingness to sacrifice once
the marriage takes place by living simply, this could well
mean the difference between children who benefit from

"hands-on" parental supervision and those who do not.

Finally, engagement is a time to take one last look at oneself and one's spouse-to-be to make doubly sure there are no impediments to the marriage.[9] Ask yourself if you respect one another as persons. Are there any obvious character flaws in the picture such as selfishness, pride, or intemperance which could interfere with what God intended to be a happy way of life? Strive to draw your partner out on all sensitive issues so that if there are differences of opinion, they will not be left to come as a surprise, perhaps even a shock, after the formal exchange of vows. At the very end of this handbook you will find 31 thought-provoking questions geared to a deeper understanding of what real communication between the parties to an engagement is all about. Hopefully, you'll read them over carefully and then discuss them individually with your husband- or wife-to-be.

If, at any point along the way, you sense something to be seriously wrong, you are morally free, indeed *morally obligated,* to terminate your relationship. A certain amount of trepidation is normal on the eve of such a momentous event. But even if, five minutes before you walk down the aisle, you have second thoughts, it is better to be safe than sorry, even with all the disappointment and embarrassment this may entail. Ten broken engagements are better than a single broken marriage. Parents, for their part, have a responsibility to make this clear to their children, regardless of how many plans they may have made or how much they may have spent.

YOUR WEDDING

There are many ways of preparing for the big day. While going over your wedding ceremony with the priest, you will want to request a nuptial Mass so that

---

9. See appendix C.

you can receive Communion in the company of any wedding guests who may be eligible. The only exception would be in the case of a mixed marriage where one might wish to avoid a display of disunity on the first day of marriage. There is usually a selection of prayers for the wedding ceremony, as well as different readings, and you are entitled to your choice. Then, too, in addition to familiarizing yourself with the ceremony itself, you will want to spend some time preparing for your role as host or hostess. Appropriately enough, bride and groom are called upon in the first formal act of their marriage to reach out to others. Some guests may have come from far away at considerable expense, and a gracious way of thanking them for their presence and support is to spend a moment or two with each of them and to have a few thoughtful words on tap. Try, if you can, to bone up in advance on guests you may not know personally.

YOUR FIRST NIGHT TOGETHER

With all that it takes to carry off a wedding reception, bride and groom may be exhausted by the end of the day, especially the bride, who generally bears the burden of preparation. Your first night is not, for this reason, a good time to apply pressure of any kind or to feel under any sense of compulsion. The more sensitive the groom in this regard, the more he will merit the esteem and confidence of his bride. The greater also will be the chance for a happy honeymoon.

HONEYMOONING

Not every couple can afford an exotic trip abroad, nor is this necessary. You will be in clover if you can get away to a place that affords some privacy, even if only for a few days, in order to relax and savor the exhilaration of new beginnings. We have all heard about harrowing honeymoons, but this happens only to those who aim to achieve too much too quickly. If you concentrate exclusively on making the other person happy in the most affectionate way you know how, neither of you will be disappointed, for it is only when one expects the lights to start flashing and the most intimate parts of a relationship to function perfectly from the very first moment that there is apt to be difficulty.

The physiological side of marriage is like a flower that takes time for all of its radiant petals to unfold. Certain forms of satisfaction may elude you for months, even years. Worry not. The marriage act is only one mode of expression among many and not necessarily the most important. Those who are truly in love will bear with delays and setbacks, confident that, in the long run, the solicitude they demonstrate for the feelings of their partner will yield fruit a hundredfold. Authentic love seeks intimacy in countless ways, and when this is the case, the sexual element has a way of falling into line. Finally, whatever you do in the course of trial and error, never lose your sense of humor. There is a side to the art of becoming one flesh that can only be described as comical, and you will find that a hearty laugh, now and then, can do wonders to put things in proper perspective.

SETTLING DOWN

The experts tell us that a partnership normally passes through three stages: (1) romance, (2) disillusionment, and (3) either a breakthrough to true love (which comes with patience and perseverance) or loneliness, distance, and pain. It is the third phase that is critical, but because its outcome depends on how the other two are understood, a look at disillusionment is in order.

Some kind of letdown following the honeymoon is almost certain to occur. Most husbands and wives find themselves hard pressed merely to cope with the strain of daily living. There may also be a gap between what is expected of marriage and what marriage as an institution is capable of delivering. Although people faced with a deteriorating relationship often believe that the fault lies with their spouse, the long and short of it is that no human being, however angelic, is equipped to guarantee the happiness of another. This is something only God Himself can do, and even He does not promise instant results. There will be periods of estrangement in even the happiest home when one or the other party is likely to feel misunderstood and dejected. There will also be intervals when a perfectly good husband or wife will drive everyone up the wall. Be patient. Wait for the sun to come out from behind those clouds. It will.

Still another reason for disillusionment is that bride and groom may discover that they have little in common. Assume, for the sake of argument, that boy meets girl on a ski trip, and they decide to get married on the basis of some fun they had on the slopes. Once they are married, there may not be any more ski trips, at least not for a while. So they settle down and find conversation awkward, decisions difficult. Suppose, in another instance, that a disproportionate amount of the couple's attention before marriage centered on ways and means of obtaining parental approval or, alternately, on the number of wedding guests to be invited and canapés to be served. After all is in place, these same people who occupied themselves with romantic plans and strategies may find themselves with few, if any, shared interests, much less common goals on which to build.

A fourth factor which helps to explain post-honeymoon blues is the effect that relaxation tends to have on human behavior. Where once we tried to look our best, we now feel free to "let our hair down." As dates, we may have been sensitive, courteous, and attentive. Now, all of a sudden, we feel we can take one another for granted.

Faults, once hidden, begin to surface under the strain of budgeting. There is a need to adjust sexually, to adapt to in-laws, and to hold down a job that overnight becomes vital to the security of two people, instead of just one. Similarly, a couple will often find that, hard as they may try, they have less uninterrupted time together once they are married, and their income may not allow for the kind of diversion or the type of wardrobe to which they were accustomed. Suddenly, they have to make decisions that are potentially divisive, and if they are not careful, they begin to lose touch. Fears, hopes, and desires go unexpressed, frustration mounts, and communication breaks down.

If you should find yourself in this situation, just remember that marriage was designed by Almighty God to last forever, and *it will* if you take your vows in good faith and with determination to go the distance. One of the answers to marital letdown in the early stages is to recognize it for what it is and to know that family harmony takes time, as well as effort.

Are there cases of chronically troubled partnerships that will resist even the most heroic efforts at healing? Yes. There may be times when marriage becomes a cross that one must carry all the way to the grave. You can be certain, however, that if this is so, it will be your ticket to Heaven. I like to think that Jesus is going to say to worn-out spouses who have persevered to the end what He said to the good thief on Calvary: *"This day thou shalt be with me in paradise"* (*Luke* 23:43). In any event, the answer is not to shop around for a new partner. Far better an imperfect union, even a separation, than the most perfect divorce. And this goes for the children, as well as the parents—especially the children. Studies indicate that it is the younger victims of divorce and remarriage who suffer the most.

But let us not dwell on the negative. Doubtless, your

match will be all you ever hoped for and more! You will seek out solutions to problems as they arise; joy will out-weigh sadness; faith will overcome all obstacles. This is the ideal, and there is no reason to believe that it is not a realizable ideal for those willing to work at it.

THE TEN COMMANDMENTS OF COMMUNICATION

Let me explain what I mean by "willing to work at it."

Who is not familiar with the soap opera stereotype of an unhappy marriage? John hides behind his newspaper when he is not glued to the tube or out drinking with the boys, while his wife, Joan, runs a chaotic household and whiles away her time on the phone with girlfriends or relatives. At the dinner table, neither party has much to say. John takes little interest in Joan's problems. She could care less about the things that occupy him at work. When they do converse over a family meal, there is more by way of criticism than positive reinforcement. So the conversation sputters along in dribs and drabs, directed mainly at the children.

According to marriage counselors, communication breakdowns such as this are not only ominous, they are also very common, affecting a broad cross-section of soci-ety. And while they may reflect a variety of marital prob-lems, they are often the cause of such problems. At the same time—and here is the rub—they are eminently avoidable. Communication is an art, and, as such, it can be cultivated. The husband and wife who communicate with ease have an automatic handle on almost any prob-lem that may arise. At the very least, they are able to grapple with ongoing challenges as a couple. There is, moreover, no reason why one can't learn communication just as one would learn any other skill.

Here, then, for those willing to work at it, are some elementary rules of thumb:

RULE 1: ***Make time for one another,*** particularly after the arrival of children. Be single-minded about setting aside a certain period each day when you can relax with your partner and unwind. It could be half an hour in the morning before the kids are up; it could be an hour in the evening after they are asleep. But it should be time you can count on since communication, to be effective, requires effort. There is much to be said for planning some sort of weekly "date." Stealing away for a meal, even if only to McDonald's, taking a leisurely stroll, or going for a relaxing drive will help to keep the dating spirit alive. If you have youngsters at home and are without a sitter, you might bring in some deli sandwiches so you can enjoy a video or TV program after the rest of the family is safely tucked away. Whatever you do, try to make the few moments you spend together as memorable and pleasant as possible.

You might also give some thought to the cultivation of leisure time activities that bring you together. I used to love the game of bridge, and although my wife, Sylvia, knew nothing about it, she was happy to take lessons. Eventually, though, she decided that bridge was not the game for her, and so we found another pastime that could be shared. By the same token, both of us used to enjoy a brisk game of tennis with partners of our own speed. Today, however, we would rather spend the little time we have rallying with one another and chasing balls for the sheer fun and fellowship of it. A couple might decide to take up an entirely new sport like bowling, again with an eye to keeping the family together. **Being** together and **staying** together are two sides of the same coin.

RULE 2: ***Take nothing for granted.*** Marital relations rarely stand still. If they don't thrive, they languish. It is important, therefore, to ask questions while keeping a hot line open to your partner at all times. In business, the boss is always checking to make sure the secretary understands what needs to be done; the attitude is one of "give me a buzz if there's a problem." So too, lifelong collaborators should be saying the same thing at every juncture, anxious to know how they are doing. There may be virtue in the "strong, silent type," but such virtue lies more in the strength than in the silence. If one party is reticent by nature, the other should not give up. The ideal couple will converse about all aspects of life, including matters of delicacy, for unless both parties can deal verbally with issues across the board, it will be hard for either of them to meet the full range of the other's needs and expectations. One might add that children, too, should have their forum. Oftentimes, parental willingness to hold a family conference for the airing of proper concerns will do wonders to restore peace and harmony.

RULE 3: ***Learn to listen*** so that others will want to confide in you. Don't get angry or upset at what you hear. Never say, "I told you so." And don't interrupt.

RULE 4: ***Be patient and discreet in drawing the other person out.*** Some spouses may want to be left alone for a spell before they open up. There may be times, too, when your partner will be talked out. At moments like this, you might decide to take a quiet walk together simply to show that you care. Whatever you do, never "dump" on a mate the moment he or she arrives home from work. Allow time for the new arrival to wash up, have a snack, and look over the mail. Time enough, later on, to catch up on the latest in your respective spheres.

RULE 5: ***Accept criticism gracefully and learn to apologize.*** Learning to take criticism is good, but better still is asking for it on occasion and being quick to apologize. The phrase "I'm sorry" is a wonderful all-purpose solvent capable of cutting through the gummiest mounds of double-talk and misunderstanding.

RULE 6: ***Avoid nagging.*** Instead of asking directly for certain favors when your wife or husband is distracted, you might consider writing a little "love note" that can be left on a desk or bureau for action when convenient. If you need something badly enough and one or two gentle reminders do not suffice, it may be time to sit down and calmly explain the urgency of the problem from your point of view. Occasionally, though, even this will not work, and you may simply have to accept what you cannot change, offering it up as a share in the Lord's suffering.

RULE 7: ***Express gratitude*** for little things, as well as big ones. There is a tendency in each of us to do exactly the opposite. Just as our better half emerges from the kitchen with a freshly baked pie, we are apt to blurt out a preference for chocolate cake. However inadvertent such remarks may be, they can put a real strain on the marriage because next in importance to the phrase "I love you" (which can never be heard too often) comes "thank you." Chances are that if we give thanks or praise ten times for every request or criticism, the ratio will be about right. Did he do a good job on the driving? Then acknowledge it. Did she put together a specially lovely floral arrangement? Then notice it.

RULE 8: ***Learn the ground rules for fighting.*** Squabbles

are a part of every marriage, and they are apt to
occur over relatively minor things. Still, they should
be kept within bounds and avoided whenever possible. Although a clearing of the air may be healthy,
loud disagreements can be destructive, as well as
exhausting, even as they tend to demoralize the
children.

While one should try to keep the lines of communication open, there is no need to confront all
prickly issues every time they arise. There is such
a thing as agreeing to disagree. Sometimes, it is the
better part of valor, when you sense a storm brewing,
to retreat, and if lightning strikes not to strike back.
Bruising your mate by calling names, shouting, or
leveling charges is almost certain to be counter-
productive.

Should you sense, at any time, that you may have
hurt your partner's feelings, intentionally or unin-
tentionally, be quick to make up. St. Paul tells us
never to let the sun go down on our anger (*Eph.*
4:26). Never go to bed angry or hurt without tender-
ing at least one kiss as a peace offering, along with
a sincere apology. We may see ourselves as the
injured party. But we can always say, "I'm sorry,
honey, if I've hurt your feelings; I didn't mean to."
Such magnanimity, coupled with a willingness to
postpone discussion, will eliminate much bitterness.
Be prompt to say you're sorry, and if you are beaten
to the punch, respond graciously. Jesus was once
asked how often one should forgive. "Seven times?"
queried Peter. "No," said Our Lord, "seventy times
seven!" (*Matt.* 18:21-22). Beyond this, once we have
forgiven, we must do our best to forget! To pout or
withhold affection after a verbal skirmish is to poi-
son the domestic atmosphere. Did you ever hear the
story about the two men who liked to discuss their
home life? One of them remarked that he loved his

wife, but every time they got into an argument, she became "historical." "You mean hysterical," said the other. "No, historical," insisted the first. "She keeps bringing up the past."

RULE 9: *Keep confidences confidential.* The best way to shut down the all-important communication process is to reveal family secrets. Some of us may feel that we are only confiding in "best friends." But once we are married, we have only one "best friend," our partner. Do not complain, especially to relatives. Bear in mind, too, that the right kind of friend will strengthen your marriage by causing you to feel satisfied, rather than dissatisfied.

RULE 10: *Use sex for the purpose intended by God.* At its best, marital intercourse can be an extraordinarily beautiful way of saying, "I love you." At its worst, it is likely to convey just the opposite meaning. One hears much these days about "having sex." What a contradiction in terms! If the procreative act is anything, it is a supreme act of *giving,* and, because it transmits the tenderest of messages in the tenderest of ways, it can be one of the most effective forms of communication. One's message will be distorted, however, if not altogether lost, if it involves manipulation or if too much emphasis is placed on the physical.

IN SUM

Chances are that if you give yourself unreservedly with one eye trained on the hereafter, your marriage will not only survive but prosper. Storms there will be, along with periods of aridity. You may be faced with a rash of catastrophes when God seems to be looking the other way. But there is no reason to panic. If you can't resolve an issue, see a mutual friend or counselor who is sound in the faith. Above all, remember that love is not a feeling that comes and goes depending upon one's mood. It is a life-long commitment which, like fine wine, improves with age. Someone once remarked that "love is what you've been through together," and how true. Perseverance is nine-tenths of the battle, and given such an attitude, com-munication crises, if and when they occur, will only bring you closer together. In the end, you will be more secure as a couple, and better off as a team, for having braved the winds of adversity.

Part 3

Family Life

Just as every person is unique, so too with families. The home you make for yourselves and for your children will differ in unexpected ways from the one in which you grew up. While it is only natural to want to duplicate one's childhood environment down to the last detail, it is also unrealistic. A man may have had a mother who fastidiously turned back his sheets every night and folded his bedspread. Now that he is married, he finds that his wife's strengths lie elsewhere. In the same way, the wife's father may have been diligent about keeping his car clean and fixing things around the house while the man she marries will let the car go for weeks without a wash. Contractors must be called in for minor repairs, and bills begin to mount. Her husband has talents of his own, but she can't help missing that paternal touch. When she asks him to take out the garbage, he does it grudgingly. Mom never put Dad to work this way. And when he requests his evening meal at 6:00 p.m., the hour to which he is accustomed, she takes offense; her family never sat down to dinner before 7:30. On top of this, she is a night owl who retires at 2:00 a.m. and likes to sleep late, while he collapses at 10:00 p.m., only to be up, bright-eyed and bushy-tailed, at 5:00 a.m.

A thousand and one similar situations, all equally petty, are likely to present themselves in the early months of marriage, and the future of the partnership may well depend on how smoothly one makes the necessary adjustments.

LEARNING TO ADAPT

Since marriage brings together people from separate and distinct backgrounds, there will be differences on almost every conceivable level. The more alike a couple is in overall values, the less the likelihood of friction. But even in the most ideal match, one partner or the other is going to be more practical in this way or that, more refined, more gregarious. One or the other will be more athletic or more artistic. Such differences can be refreshing because "opposites attract." Nevertheless, along with such discrepancy comes a need to hone the skill of conciliation which, in turn, requires communication.

Let us assume, for instance, that after love-making, a husband's mood shifts, and his wife, who is slower to disengage, feels abandoned. Hopefully, she will confide in him, and he will meet her more than half way when he senses that her feelings in this regard are more intense than his. Perhaps, in another type of situation, the wife, who was schooled by her family to conduct lengthy post-mortems after every social event, is married to a man who feels ill at ease raking company over the coals the moment the party is over. He reveals his sensitivity to her when she is in a receptive mood, and if she finds that her feelings run less deeply than his, she acts accordingly. In a similar scenario, the husband may be the type who was taught to verbalize disagreements and talk everything out on the spot. His wife, on the other hand, is accustomed to letting a good deal go and to warding off confrontation. In this instance, Mr. "Settle-it-right-away" will demonstrate a willingness to defer the moment of truth, while Mrs. "Talk-about-it-later" will address more issues head-on.

Some of this may sound picayune, but it is the stuff of which separations and divorces are made. Unless there is some great moral principle at stake, don't hesitate to be the one who does the yielding.

And what, perchance, if both parties prove adamant? Toss a coin or work out a formula. In the case of the night owl and early bird, she might go to bed a couple of hours earlier than usual while he might retire a couple of hours later, and if she doesn't fall right off to sleep, she will read a book while he accustoms himself to sleeping with the light on. Or take something as simple as the evening meal. Suppose he is always watching TV or tinkering with the car when she calls him to dinner—by the time he reaches the table, the main course is cold. This is something an experienced couple will try to resolve at an opportune time. Possibly, as part of the bargain, she will agree to serve her summons earlier with a "Honey, dinner will be ready in five minutes," while he, for his part, will make more of an effort to pry himself loose. Different couples facing different problems will hit upon different solutions. The main thing is for each couple to be imaginative in coping with the challenges that are sure to come their way.

TRADITIONAL AND NON-TRADITIONAL ROLES

In today's world, where women are often employed full-time outside the home, some equitable way must be found to share domestic duties. It may be that if one party balances the checkbook, empties waste baskets, and cleans the bathroom, the other will vacuum and dust. Any division of labor will do so long as it is fair and efficient.

Husbands and wives are capable of doing a great many things traditionally reserved for the opposite sex, and doing them well. However, there is always the danger, in an age of accelerated social change and experimentation, that one will go overboard. So don't hesitate to backtrack should you find yourself departing from the norm established by your parents. She may say she doesn't mind going to a filling station with the car; he may insist that he doesn't mind cooking; both may be sincere. Yet within a short while, both may yearn inwardly for a more conventional lifestyle. Tradition did not become tradition by accident!

THE SPIRIT OF PARTNERSHIP

Marriage thrives on husbandly, as well as wifely, deference. Although Scripture makes it clear that wives should be submissive toward their husbands, relying on them for leadership in the broadest sense of the word, it also says that husbands should love their wives as they love their own bodies and as Christ loves His Church. For the man, such love implies tender solicitude and steady support, along with frequent consultation. The wife, who is his equal in dignity before God, deserves a voice in all family decisions, especially those that affect her directly. But beyond the question of rights, her input on a wide range of issues will be useful. Two heads are commonly better than one, and she is bound to be more knowledgeable in certain areas than her husband.

True, he is head of the household and, like the chairman of the board of a corporation, responsible for the smooth running and overall well-being of the family. But this does not mean that he has to take personal charge of all areas, especially when his wife may be better qualified. It also assumes that he is in possession of his faculties and capable of demonstrating conjugal love of the type described by St. Paul. In the case of absentee husbands and fathers, the woman may find herself forced by default to step into the breach. But this is neither the norm nor the ideal. The good wife will encourage her husband even if he is less than perfect, just as she will consult regularly and give careful thought to his opinion.

Husbandly solicitude could mean attending to the children while she goes to a meeting. It might call for doing the dishes when he would rather be watching a ball game on TV. Whatever the case, if each partner tries to make things easier and more pleasant for the other, volunteering on occasion to tackle unpleasant chores, even to the point of friendly argument—call it a "heavenly argument"—if each strives to give the other the better portion in life, there will be little danger of marital breakdown.

Husbandly "headship" is a notion that is touched upon by both Peter and Paul, the latter at least three separate times, suggesting that it may have been as hot an issue in those days as it is today.[10] Obviously, women have entered many fields formerly reserved for men, and some have assumed the role of breadwinner. This, in itself, however, does not alter the dynamics of conjugal interaction. Suppose, in a comparable situation, that the father of a particular family were to fall ill. His teenage son might have to drop out of school and find employment to help support his parents. But regardless of what the son did or didn't do, he would still be the son and, as such, obligated to show filial respect and obedience.

KEEPING THE DATING SPIRIT ALIVE

Marriage, like courtship, flourishes in an atmosphere of small, voluntary attentions. A rose wrapped in baby's breath that one brings home unexpectedly with a card

---

10. *1 Cor.* 11:3, 9; *Col.* 3:18; *Titus* 2:5; *1 Peter* 3:1-7. See also *Genesis* 2:18 and 3:16. *Arcanum Divinae Sapientiae* (1880) by Leo XIII calls man "the ruler of the family." Pius XI, in *Casti Connubii* (1930) quoted Leo XIII and alluded to the husband's "chief place in ruling" (sec. 2). And John Paul II, in *Familiaris Consortio*, refers to the "superiority of male prerogatives," even as he condemns "machismo" (sec. 25). According to the *Catechism of the Catholic Church* (1994), man and woman were "created for one another," and each can be helpmate to the other; but woman was specially given by God to man "as a 'helpmate'" (sec. 1605).

saying, "I love you more and more every day," can mean a lot; so, too, can an occasional phone call from work to say, "I miss you," or an affectionate note slipped surreptitiously into the family mailbox. A special dish or, if time permits, a special meal would make an equally nice surprise.

Trying to please one another in little things implies courtesy and consideration. If, while dating, the man was polite enough to pause, before starting a meal, so that his fiancée could be the first to start, if he held her coat for her or helped her into automobiles, then he should do the same as her husband. If, along parallel lines, she deferred to him in public and took pains to look her best, she can be sure that such things will continue to make him happy. Some of the social graces and amenities commonplace a generation or two ago may have vanished. But the general idea of courtship, whether in or out of marriage, remains as valid as ever.

Go out of your way to be positive. Refrain from reminiscing about old flames, and don't dignify temptations against the Sixth Commandment by confessing them to your spouse. Keep your eyes under control and your heart under strict lock and key at all times, striving for a loyalty that is 100 percent. If, by chance, someone of the opposite sex should happen to attract you in a serious way, do not confide in such a person. Avoid unnecessary contact, and you'll be amazed at how quickly the problem disappears. You may not be doing anything that is technically wrong, but people are bound to talk, and such talk can spread. Discretion calls for the elimination of undue familiarity with anyone who could pose as a rival for your affection. As Father Frank Lee puts it, "Marriage does not simply bring two people together; it also excludes any third person. A word to the wise—everybody wants to be mature and sophisticated and modern and a few other big words, but we are still little human beings who are very jealous of our treasures."[11]

NO SECOND GUESSING

Imagine a home in which the husband forgets to put the cap back on his toothpaste after brushing. Time and again, she reminds him; time and again he forgets. Finally, one morning, she awakes to find the tube perfectly capped. He has mended his ways! But her first reaction is, "Honey, how come you aren't brushing your teeth anymore?" No one likes to be second-guessed.

GIVING THE BENEFIT OF THE DOUBT

How would you react if you found yourself on the receiving end of a miscarriage, birth defect, or inability to conceive? Can there be any such thing as a "mistake" or misfortune when it comes to products of divine engineering? Granted, it requires faith to accept what God sends, or fails to send, and to see in childlessness (or parenthood under difficult circumstances) a divinely appointed mission on a par with any other. But without such faith we fall prey to groundless feelings of guilt. Childlessness may involve some deficiency on the part of the woman, but there are times when it can be traced to the man. It is best, therefore, not to jump to conclusions. Even in situations where something or someone is clearly lacking, the partner who is truly in love will respond with the charity St. Paul had in mind when he wrote that *"love is patient, love is kind...*[it] *bears with all things, believes all things, hopes all things, endures all things"* (*1 Cor.* 13:4-7).

The Bible tells of an exemplary husband, Elcana, whose barren wife, Anna, was given to continual weep-

---

11. Liguori Publications, Sunday flyer for 28 December 1975.

ing over her condition. Elcana could have compounded Anna's grief by dismissing her. Instead, he pleads endearingly, *"Am I not better to thee than ten children?"* Elcana and Anna were eventually blessed with the birth of a son, Samuel, who went on to become one of the world's most celebrated prophets (*1 Sam.* 1). Elcana discovered that the Lord had a package on the shelf which He had delayed delivering, and there was ample reason to rejoice. Still, from the Christian standpoint, he was not so much released from sadness as simply introduced to a different kind of happiness with a whole new set of joys and sorrows, risks and responsibilities.

RIGHT TO PRIVACY

It may seem like a small point, but one can easily forget that married people have just as much of a right to privacy as anyone else. Even the most gregarious individual will appreciate a moment or two, now and then, to read, meditate, or simply to relax. Not all homes are spacious enough to afford a den or a sewing room, but there should be some kind of haven to which one can retreat without fear of intrusion. It might even be a desk or a sofa, as long as it is viewed as "off limits" when certain persons occupy it at certain times. The amazing thing is that children can be just as cooperative in this regard as grown-ups once they understand the reason why.

YOUNGSTERS AND DISCIPLINE

Not surprisingly, it is the little ones who tend to be most malleable. From the moment of birth, they are gifted with a quite remarkable sense of right and wrong, and you will find that, with persistence on your part, along with a reasonable system of rewards and punishments, they take rather well to discipline, at times almost demanding it. Aside from food and rest, children are hungry for two things above all else: discipline and affection, and they need them in equal proportion. If they are not kissed, held, hugged, indulged on occasion, and listened to, they will find it hard to obey; and if they don't obey, they won't remain huggable or kissable for long. Appearances notwithstanding, each of them, deep down, also likes to be told in a tactful way what to do and how to do it. Gradually, and with patience, they can be taught to behave with restraint, courtesy, and consideration, and when this happens, they add immeasurably to the joy of home life. If, on the other hand, they are permitted to roam and rummage at will, to jump, scream, and disturb the neighbors, if their unruliness begins to drive a wedge between the parties responsible for their welfare, as it surely will, they are going to be the first to suffer.

A smooth-running household coupled with proper management of the children are integral to the whole notion of Christian generosity in procreation. How can parents be disposed to welcome more children if those they already have are a constant nuisance? How can they make time for a larger family if their daily schedule is already a shambles or if their lines of communication have broken down?

Since every child is unique, the key to wholesome discipline lies in knowing what to expect from each as an individual and taking the time to find out. Obviously, they should not be punished for doing what they cannot help or for failing to measure up to an unreasonably high standard—infants with severe gastrointestinal pain are going to cry; babies, when they teethe, are going to drool, some of them like Niagara Falls! But it is never a mistake to aim high. Experienced parents know how often youngsters are likely to surprise them by accomplishing the "impossible."

As to method, most would agree that corporal punishment should be held to a minimum. Some children are so docile that an occasional verbal reprimand is all they need. For the majority, however, a timely slap on the hand or a spanking administered dispassionately will do a world of good.

"Spare the rod and spoil the child," one of the better-known passages from Scripture (*Prov.* 13:24), was embellished in a humorous vein by the late Archbishop Fulton Sheen, who quipped, "No child is ever hurt by an occasional pat on the back as long as it is given low enough and hard enough." Clearly, there are limits to what can be achieved under any system. Too much punishment may be worse than none at all. At the same time, one seldom hears an adult taking his parents to task for having been too strict, assuming they were conscientious and set a good example. Dwight D. Eisenhower grew up in a family of six boys. All were exposed to the often erratic temper and leather strap of a strict father. Yet there was not a single black sheep in the fold.

One of the most positive techniques is to have children help out around the house so they can learn the value of honest work and experience the joy of giving. At the earliest age, they are incredibly eager to be helpful, perhaps sensing the relationship between work and maturity. Whatever the reason, a skillful parent will foster this eagerness by assigning appropriate tasks and taking time to encourage children in their effort.

Finally, because parents represent the justice, as well as the mercy, of God, it behooves them to be truthful and to avoid even the appearance of favoritism. At the same time, by agreeing privately on matters of discipline, they will avoid the temptation to fight and countermand one another's orders before the children. Tykes, always quick to find chinks in the parental armor, can be mercilessly exploitative.

THE BEAUTY OF SCHEDULES

You may be one of those who is temperamentally averse to any form of structure or regimentation. But if you are open to suggestion along this line, there is much to be said for family routine. If nothing else, it maximizes the time at your disposal and gives everyone a heightened sense of belonging. As long as meal time is anyone's guess and the whereabouts of family members a mystery, there is bound to be some lag in morale. Conversely, when a definite time is set aside for dinner, as well as for cleaning, laundry, shopping, church-going, and family outings, young and old will be able to plan accordingly. Children, especially, will benefit from having a regular agenda if they are to complete their homework, attend to chores, and say their prayers. I can still remember how happy our daughter, Mary Anne, was at the age of four when we invited her to join us in saying the last decade of the evening Rosary. Thereafter, at exactly the appointed time, she wanted nothing so much as to set up the holy card, along with the beads, and watch the candle being lit. In fact, she would remind us if we forgot!

The more children there are at home, the greater the need to ensure that each of them receives a daily quota of "quality time." Those of school age will be fortunate if they are limited in their access to TV. They will also have set bed times, along with sufficient exercise during the day to keep them in a prone position at night.

When all is said and done, personal sacrifice is the glue that is going to hold your brood together. Once you march down that aisle, consider yourself more or less on permanent duty. It may be tempting to dodge family cares for a while and go off on your own. You may even be tempted to run home, ostrich-like, to father and mother. But prudence dictates otherwise. Everyone benefits from an occasional time-out, and if you can afford babysitting, or if there is someone trustworthy who is willing to spell you, then by all means escape. But the children will be grown before you know it, and, in the early stages, they stand to benefit enormously from every moment you spend with them. I needn't add that when you and your partner do go away, it is advisable to spend the time together. Separate vacations are not, on the whole, very constructive.

BUDGETING

Your goal here should be to save as much as you can for education and retirement. Such providence will serve as a hedge against sudden illness while leaving the door open to generosity in matters of procreation. If husband and wife both have a career outside the home and it seems advisable, with the passage of time and the growth of the family, for one of them to leave full-time work (or to quit altogether) so that he or she can assume primary care of the children, this ought to be an option. In no case should the "homemaker" spouse be *forced* to work outside the home. Such a decision, if taken, should be taken jointly, and the work should be such that it can be scaled back or discontinued in the event that it poses a threat to the family. Based on Christian principles, it is far better to live with only two or three outfits in one's closet than to short-change those whose life-long welfare depends in so many instances on your watchful presence.

The actual budget takes time, but it is not all that difficult and will repay all the effort you put into it. First, jot down your fixed expenses for the year. For example: rent or mortgage payments, insurance premiums, telephone bills, automobile depreciation, utilities, taxes, haircuts, cleaners, laundry, and cosmetics. Items like rent, which are normally calculated on a monthly basis, should be multiplied by twelve to arrive at the yearly cost. There may be other regular items depending on your situation (visits to the dentist or eye doctor, transportation to work, and so forth). Charitable contributions, along with outlays for the support of the parish, should be at the very top of one's list of "fixed" expenses. Anyone who can afford a pizza or a movie once in a while can drop at least this much into the collection basket on Sunday. Remember the parable of the widow's mite (_Mark_ 12:41-44). You will find it useful, in addition, to have a category called "miscellaneous," still under the heading of fixed expenses. This will allow for freak occurrences such as emergency repairs and replacement of appliances. Expect the unexpected, and budget for it.

Next, draw up a list of flexible items, again figuring on a twelve-month basis: food, clothing, savings, recreation, entertainment, vacations, magazine and newspaper subscriptions, gifts, and the like. If, after adding up all the expenses on both lists, you find that a single income is insufficient, you should begin paring down the figures on each list, especially on list #2, until you arrive at a satisfactory balance.

As we all know, the best way to save is not to spend, which means purchasing only what is absolutely necessary at reasonable prices. If you are the type who cannot resist bargains unrelated to immediate family needs, bring an itemized list to the supermarket to avoid impulse buying. Otherwise, you will be on the road to the poor house. Beware of installment plans. No one can ever be sure what kind of demand the future is going to make on a family's income. Many who rely on credit wind up paying exorbitant sums of interest for the privilege of deferring payment on goods they should never have bought in the first place. Look out, too, for "Ma Bell." She can kill you by turning 35¢ into $35 when you are not looking. Be sure also to use a check book. Balance it every month, and pay by check or credit card as often as possible, especially when purchasing substantial items. In this way, you'll have an itemized record of where your money is going when it comes time to plan next year's budget. Save bank and credit card statements for a full year, if possible, and cancelled checks for ten. You never know when you may need to produce them for insurance purposes or the IRS.

As for who holds the purse strings, they should be jointly held in most cases. Congenital spendthrifts exist, but they are rare. Likewise when it comes to deciding how to dispose of family income. The mere fact that you are bound by a budget will render certain decisions automatic, and the ones that are not should be subject to compromise based on who feels more strongly. If each party bends a little, neither will be on the losing end. Most of the time, when finances pose a serious problem, the source of the difficulty can be traced to a lack of love.

In-Laws

However much two families may have in common, they will not react to all situations in exactly the same way any more than they will share the same expectations. On a purely practical level, they are likely to have different ways of celebrating religious feasts and holidays. Feelings can run deep as to how many presents should be exchanged at Christmas and when they should be opened. Familiarity breeds contempt, and parents of the bride and groom, while not intending it, can easily come between husband and wife.

Don't misunderstand. Some couples, when they marry, develop a wonderful relationship with their new families. Grandparents are a godsend. They can be extremely generous. And who can forget the story of Ruth, an Old Testament widow, who assured her mother-in-law that *"where you go I will go, and where you lodge I will lodge; your people shall be my people and your God my*

God" (*Ruth* 1:16). In-laws deserve the greatest respect and consideration. At the very least, we should avoid criticizing them, especially in the presence of our mate, when in so doing we may be treading on a loyalty that is as deeply rooted as it is natural. Even if the criticism strikes a sympathetic chord, it will put one's partner in an awkward spot.

At the same time, it has been well said that "in-laws are outlaws." Like all adages, this one may not ring entirely true in every circumstance, but it contains a wealth of wisdom. Scripture has it that *"a man shall leave his mother and father and cling to his wife and the two shall become one flesh"* (*Gen.* 2:24). In any dispute, therefore, pitting spouse against in-law (or blood relative, for that matter), the spouse's mate should remain neutral or, preferably, come down on the side of his or her partner. Likewise, if a parent requires correction, the person to do it is the blood relative. We are enjoined by the Fourth Commandment to honor father and mother, but our primary allegiance is to the person we marry, and couples who experience friction with their relatives are advised to limit the contact. If and when in-laws offer advice, the prudent response is, "Thank you for your thoughtfulness; I'll talk it over with my better half." Never complain, and never tolerate remarks or behavior from family members that denigrate your spouse, even indirectly. As mentioned earlier, smooth communication between husband and wife is essential to the health of the marriage, and this calls for 100 percent loyalty.

FAMILY FRIENDS

When it comes to friends, it is well to adopt a similar attitude, subordinating personal attachments to the larger goal of a secure and happy home. Following the wedding, one or both spouses may have to forge new ties if they find their partner ill at ease with long-time associates or, as sometimes happens, overly fond of them.

Friendship between married couples is an especially dicey proposition since all four of the parties must like, or at least not dislike, each of the persons on the other side; and along with the liking, there must be an absence of romantic attachment. Generally speaking, the friends you cultivate should share your underlying values. Christian hospitality has a place, and good fellowship is again something to be cherished, but neither has anything to do with opening your home to people whose behavior is scandalous or whose offspring may prejudice your family's chance to mature in an environment that is morally safe and culturally stimulating.[12]

THE CHILDREN'S EDUCATION

Parents have the right, as well as the duty, to educate their children, especially in matters of faith and morals.[13] This calls for a strict censorship of TV, film, and theater programs, many of which are slanted in such a way as to undermine the Catholic ideal of marriage. When they are not downright filthy, they often present abortion, adultery, and remarriage after divorce as perfectly acceptable, if not praiseworthy.

Another responsibility that is part and parcel of Catholic parenting is the fostering of religious vocations. This is not something that can be left to chance. If good priests and nuns, sisters and brothers, are not included in the

---

12. See appendix B for the Scriptural basis.
13. Vatican Council II, *Gravissimum educationis,* sec. 3. According to the *Catechism* (1994), parents, not the state, "have the primary responsibility for the procreation and education of their children." They are "the principal and first educators of their children," and "the fundamental task of marriage and the family is to be at the service of life" (sections 1653 and 2372). Parents also have the right to choose a school for their offspring "which corresponds to their own convictions" (sec. 2229).

family circle of friends, how are youngsters to find role models? How often, in our secular materialistic culture, do we hear the frivolous parental boast that little Johnny, aged five, "has a girlfriend"? This is a perfect example of what *not* to do. According to Vatican Council II, "No pressure, direct or indirect, should be put on the young to make them enter marriage or choose a specific partner."[14]

Responsible parenthood also calls for the placing of children in a wholesome intellectual environment commensurate with their ability. Most importantly, it means making sure that they receive the right instruction in such Christian virtues as modesty, temperance, and purity. It is far more important that they turn out to be men and women of character than that they be erudite, though the two goals can be mutually reinforcing. There is a tendency to assume that, when youngsters are sent off to Catholic schools, they will receive all that they need in this area, but not necessarily. It all depends on the institution. Some Catholic schools and colleges do an excellent job of instructing students in the fundamentals of their faith. Others do not. Consequently, parents must be well informed about the school curriculum in order to supplement or counteract it when necessary. It goes without saying that the ideal place for sons and daughters to learn "the facts of life" is at home, where their teachers, Mom and Dad, practice what they preach. But if it has to be at school, one should know precisely what is being taught and how. In certain situations, one may have to go a step further and request that a child be excused from class.

In recent years, the moral caliber of public, and even private, education has declined sharply, and an increasing number of families have turned to home schooling. Not every parent is properly equipped for this kind of

---

14. Vatican Council II, *Gaudium et Spes,* sec. 52.

work—it is difficult under the best of circumstances. On the other hand, there is obviously much to be said for a system that affords such a high degree of control over content, as well as a merciful side-stepping of astronomical tuition bills. There are also some very good programs available, complete with texts, workbooks, parent manuals, and phone hot lines (see appendix K).

A Bright and Cheerful Home

Shifting the focus for just a moment, you have undoubtedly thought about the kind of home you want—one that is bright, clean, and reasonably in order, as well as comfortable and inviting to members of the family. Just so. There is no need for slavish imitation of all the stylish models featured in picture magazines. But there are things one can do by way of decoration and furnishing to make the place where you live "Home, Sweet Home." Even the way you get yourself up can make a difference. As far as personal appearance is concerned, a moment or two before the mirror, now and then, will be time well spent. A quick touch of the comb, an occasional dash of cold water on the face, or a fresh outfit will add to the domestic ambiance, and this goes for both spouses. To be sure, home is a place to relax and unwind. But it should also be a pleasant place, pleasant enough for family members to miss when they are away for any length of time.

Poverty, Chastity, and Obedience

Doubtless you are familiar with the three vows taken by men and women who enter the religious life: poverty, chastity, and obedience. But have you ever considered that similar conditions apply to the married state as well?

Chastity, not to be confused with virginity or celibacy, is a matter of keeping one's sexual appetite under control within the limits set by God, and as such it is likely to pose as much of a challenge to the married person as it does to the nun or priest. In marriage, such factors as physical absence, pregnancy, lack of privacy, domestic strife, and even nervous exhaustion can be formidable barriers to self-expression and therefore to chastity. Celibacy, on the other hand, which calls for constant restraint, may be less difficult precisely because it is constant.

Chastity calls for modesty in dress and behavior, just as it excludes anything that might give rise to scandal or lead to an adulterous relationship. Clearly, there are many ways of sinning against the Sixth Commandment: by what one says, by one's body language, by what one communicates through the eyes (*Matt.* 5:28). In Leo Tolstoy's masterpiece, *Anna Karenina,* an attractive young woman (Anna) who is married to an elder statesman, decides to travel some distance in order to help her brother put his affairs in order. En route, at a railway station, she catches sight of a dashing young army officer by the name of Vronsky. Turning on the platform to give him a second look, she commits a fatal indiscretion, for in that split second, a romantic attachment is conceived which leads to the birth of an illegitimate child. In the end, a desperately unhappy Anna throws herself in the path of an oncoming steam locomotive.

The prudent spouse will consider whether lunch with a business associate of the opposite sex has to be a private affair or whether it can be arranged as more of an official function in an impersonal setting. There will also be times when one's daily routine may call for adjustment in order to avoid a too friendly colleague, knowing that one thing can lead to another.

In short, prudence and discretion are golden in marriage just as they are in the religious life. Shakespeare's play, *Othello,* focuses on the machinations of the wicked Iago, who manages to convince Othello that the latter's wife, Desdemona, has been unfaithful with Cassio. Desdemona may be innocent, but she is also imprudent, for on her honeymoon, no less, she prods Othello into reinstating Cassio, thereby fueling her husband's suspicion. It makes no difference that her solicitude for Cassio springs from unselfish motives. She has been indiscreet, and it is the indiscretion that seals her fate.

Poverty, second of the three vows, has less to do with some federally designated minimum standard of living than with a Christ-like spirit of detachment. How much in the way of material goods does one need to be happy? The more possessions we have, the more we worry, and the more complicated our life becomes. Imposing homes and costly appointments, because they require continual care, can place heavy demands on our limited store of time and energy. Tolstoy's short story, "How Much Land Does a Man Need?" tells of a man who spends every waking moment of his life acquiring real estate. On reaching a certain section of the country, he is told that for a given sum he can secure title to all the land he is able to stake out on foot in a single day. Pleased, he starts off early in the morning at a frenzied pace, darting here and there to lay claim to the choicest parcels. As the sun begins to set, however, he is still far afield with much unfinished business, and in one last, desperate effort to complete his survey, he collapses from sheer exhaustion and falls dead at the feet of the owners, who promptly dig him a hole six feet deep by three feet wide.

How much land does a man need? Christian detachment calls for a life of simplicity in keeping with the station to which one is called, and simplicity, in turn, opens the door to generosity. I shall never forget the title of a sermon I once saw posted outside a small church in Manhattan: "To Live Simply That Others May Simply Live."

One way of practicing economy is to refrain from impulse buying. Some couples seem to feel they must furnish their home all at once. Why so? By waiting for sales and shopping at a more leisurely pace, one will have a better sense for what is available, and the pieces that turn up along the way may be more to one's liking. Tastes and needs can change, and if our friends think less of us for living modestly, then perhaps we should find some new friends.

Obedience, the third of the above-mentioned vows, implies a readiness to yield in matters of personal preference, and again, it applies as much to the home as it does to the rectory. It has little to do with playing doormat and everything to do with Christian deference. Does your mate feel strongly about a particular charitable cause? Then contribute. Does your partner have a better sense for where to hang pictures? Be grateful. And if you are the one with the better sense, you can still go along in the interest of equanimity. Does your spouse complain about being lonely or neglected? Perhaps your job is working too much of a hardship on the home. It may be time to rearrange your schedule or find a new position. All of us are obliged to do an honest day's work for an honest day's pay. In fact, it is our Christian *duty* to excel in every way possible. But having said this, we must not forget that the welfare of our family comes first, and conjugal obedience means doing whatever it takes to foster a spirit of husbandly and wifely solicitude.

THE MISSIONARY SPIRIT

It is easy to overlook the importance of the ordinary home as a missionary outpost. We live in a world controlled by sceptics and non-believers, and although history testifies to prodigious feats of conversion accomplished in faraway places like India, Africa, and Latin

America, there is a burning need for missionaries right now here at home. Today's "heathen" are more apt to be rich than poor, educated than uneducated. Many of them attend Sunday Mass out of a knee-jerk respect for tradition or ethnic ritual, and we may be the only serious Catholics they ever meet. Uninformed when it comes to Church teaching, they pick and choose, cafeteria style, among various rules and precepts. Some will tell you that it doesn't really matter what one believes so long as one is "sincere." Poor souls. They need to ask themselves why Jesus died, why He commissioned the apostles to preach to all nations, and why thousands of Christians in every age have sacrificed their lives for what they believe.

Vatican Council II stressed that if we are to offer an example of family living that is attractive, if we are to advertise our love for Jesus, if we are going to answer questions that come our way, we must familiarize ourselves with the fundamentals of the faith on an adult level. This could call for attendance at a Bible class, for more regular reading and meditation on sacred scripture, or for dipping more deeply into the lives of the martyrs and saints. Another approach might be to subscribe to Catholic newspapers and magazines such as *The Catholic Answer, Catholic Heritage, Catholic Digest, Catholic Twin Circle, Our Sunday Visitor, The Wanderer, The Catholic Parent,* and the *National Catholic Register.* When religious instruction terminates at the age of twelve or thirteen, as is generally the case, one may boast all one wants of a college education, but in the area that counts most, one continues to function at an elementary school level. Religious education is a continual, life-long process.

Returning, though, to the domestic front, will TV be enshrined as the high altar of your home? Will you select a Playboy air freshener for your car or something more in keeping with what you profess to believe? A friend of mine used to have a tiny cactus on his desk as a reminder of Christ's crown of thorns, one of many ways he had hit upon to stay in touch with reality.

We should ask ourselves how guests are going to know that ours is a Catholic home and that we care about the salvation of souls. Will their eye be drawn to a crucifix or some other object of religious art that has special meaning for us?

How will you and your family celebrate Sundays and holy days? Will they be different from regular days in the sense of avoiding unnecessary shopping and employ- ment? Is Mass going to be something to be gotten out of the way as quickly as possible as your troop arrives late in cutoffs and sneakers and then leaves early, or will you be prepared physically, mentally, and spiritually for God's dinner party? Will Easter be reduced to chocolate eggs and bunnies, or will there be some reminder of the Christian dimension? How do you propose to reflect on the meaning of the Cross and Resurrection? In short, how are you going to "keep the faith" and foster religious vocations, a responsibility that rests as much with the laity as it does with nuns and priests?

Will you keep a small library of spiritual classics side- by-side with the Bible, and will your children have access to inspirational works suitable for their age? The Daugh- ters of St. Paul publish an excellent series on the lives of the saints. Highly recommended, too, is *The Imitation of Christ* by Thomas á Kempis, *Introduction to the Devout and Holy Life* by St. Francis de Sales, and *The Way* by Blessed Josemaría Escrivá de Balaguer. Fulton Oursler and Archbishop Fulton Sheen wrote first-rate biographies of Christ. What one reads has much to do with what kind of person one is, as well as with the type of person one is likely to become.

Part 4

Spirituality

When one hears the familiar words, "for better or for worse, for richer or for poorer, in sickness and in health," one tends to think of material concerns, the ups and downs of the stock market, or a bout with the flu. But another and more significant side of these vows is their supernatural content. There will be "dark nights of the soul." In the end, God will ask each of us if we have made it easier or harder for our spouse to get to Heaven, and as a consequence, we need to be spiritually involved.

Spirituality is a hard word to define. I remember one of my college roommates saying that he would like to marry a saint. When I asked him why, he replied that a saint is a person who is not only happy but also capable of making others happy. At the time, his words were simply words—I had only the vaguest sense of what he was driving at. Today, though, after having pulled in harness with a sterling partner for more than twenty-five years, I can appreciate the clarity of his vision.

Some of the world's greatest saints were in fact married, among them Thomas More of England, Louis IX of France, Monica (mother of St. Augustine), Margaret Clitherow of York, Isidore of Madrid, Margaret of Scotland, and Frances of Rome, not to mention the Holy Family and John's parents, Zachary and Elizabeth. So there is no dearth of role models.

Saints are not born; they are made, many of them later in life. If one reads the story of St. Augustine or St. Ignatius of Loyola, one finds that both of them were way-

51

ward as young men, but once they experienced the saving grace of conversion, they sped upward at a breathtaking pace to the very pinnacle of perfection. Was it easy? St. Paul likens the quest for spirituality to the running of a race, and races are exhausting (*1 Cor.* 9:24 and *2 Tim.* 4:7). But if devotees of physical fitness can engage in aerobics, jogging, dieting, and body building at all hours of the day and night, why shouldn't we go out of our way to do some of the things recommended for fitness of soul?

Neither my wife nor I would ever claim to be saints. Far from it. Traveling together on life's journey, we can look back on our share of flat tires. The Lord has had to put up with an awful lot from me in particular, and He still does! The two of us have been on the road long enough, however, to know that there are a number of practical, down-to-earth measures which can help a family stay the course, and the first of these is prayer.

PRAYER

Exxon Corporation used to advertise its brand of gasoline as the one that would "put a tiger in your tank." We, too, need to put a tiger in our tank, and one of the ways of doing this, I have found, is through prayer.

Motoring through some of the rural areas of Ohio, my wife and I used to see billboards with a homey message: "The family that prays together stays together." It struck a sympathetic chord because we knew it to be true. Christ said the same thing, of course, when He promised that *"Whatever you ask in my name you shall receive,"* and *"Wherever two or three are gathered in my name, there am I in their midst"* (*Matt.* 7:7-11; 18:19-20). With God, all things are possible, provided they are pleasing in His sight, and one of the most pleasing is a love affair between a man and a woman that never ends.

When the priest asked Johnny if he said his prayers

every night before going to bed, Johnny responded, "Yes, Father." "And do you also say them when you wake up in the morning?" continued the padre. "No, Father." "And why not, Johnny?" Came the confident answer: "'Cause I ain't never scared during the day!" All of us have a bit of the Johnny in us. We fall to our knees on the death of a sweetheart or at the onset of terminal cancer, and the rest of the time we are content to coast, forgetting that it is the events of everyday life that make or break a marriage and that the same source of strength invoked in times of extreme difficulty is available to us every day of the week.

Most of us pray at set times such as early in the morning, at meal time, and again before turning in. Without question, such prayer—call it formal prayer if you will—can be rewarding. At the same time, there is something to be said for praying in a less formal manner. Not that one approach precludes the other. On the contrary, St. Paul tells us to pray "at all times" (*Eph.* 6:18; *1 Thess.* 5:17), which means that we should learn to engage in Heavenly chit-chat while mowing the lawn and doing the dishes.

A typical conversation might go something like this: "Well, Lord, here I am again rocking the baby on my chest and applying hot compresses to her aching ear. She's in such pain! But I know that You're there and won't abandon us. I know, too, that You'll have other assignments for me. Can You see the smile on my face? It makes me happy to think that all of this is for You." Or suppose you're in a traffic jam and you exclaim, "Lord, what a mess! I'm not complaining, but why have You got me sandwiched in here bumper-to-bumper? Because You miss hearing from me on normal occasions? Is there something deep down in my life that needs correcting? So that's it!"

St. Teresa of Avila, as jolly a soul as ever lived, traveled the highways and byways of Spain on any number of occasions, all in the service of God. Transportation was primitive in those days, and once, after her carriage overturned crossing a stream, she burst out, "Lord, if this is the way You treat Your friends, no wonder You have so few of them!" Like Teresa, we should go to God as we are, thinking about all that He has reserved for us in Heaven and jotting down some of the things we plan to do when we get there.

Prayer can have interesting side effects. As a writer, I used to be annoyed by library patrons who coughed with such maddening regularity that it seemed they wanted everyone in the room to notice them. On other occasions, I was galled by the sound of car alarms going off under my office window. The only solution that worked, I found, was to say a Hail Mary every time I heard a cough or car alarm. Let me tell you, no church bell or Angelus could have been more effective as a call to meditation. And with what results! Not only did my prayer life improve; my writing perked up, my spirits revived, and I soon reached the point of looking forward to the next interruption! Just think how different life would be if the average supermarket clerk or toll collector in large, impersonal cities like New York, where rudeness is the rule, came to view everyday work as their ticket to Heaven, rather than as a form of drudgery. In place of sourpusses, we would have a legion of smiling angels.

The application to marriage should be clear. Prayer is a form of communication, and once we learn to communicate with God, we will be that much more effective at reaching our spouse. If nothing else, the two indispensable phrases, "I love you" and "I'm sorry," will be quicker to roll off our lips because we will be saying them over and over to the Lord.

THE SACRAMENTS

Next to prayer, and just as important for keeping a "tiger in the tank," are three very special sacraments: Penance (the Sacrament of Reconciliation or Confession), Holy Communion, and Matrimony itself. Together, they open the sluice gates of a spiritual reservoir from which one can draw down inexhaustible energy and inspiration.

Matrimony

Matrimony, to begin in reverse order, is more than a contract in which bride and groom pledge to accept one another for better or worse. It is also a solemn covenant between the couple and God, as well as between the couple and society, and as such, it carries with it a mighty reserve of spiritual power to assist us in the discharge of our conjugal duties. Fortunately, such grace, conferred during the wedding ceremony, remains a constant source of strength.

Scripture tells us vividly of the importance Christ attached to marriage. He likened His kingdom to a marriage feast, chose a wedding celebration at Cana as the occasion for His first public miracle, and selected a humble family to be the instrument of His salvation. God could have come to us in a variety of ways. What is remarkable is that He chose to come through the womb of a woman and was raised, like any other child, by a father and mother. Presumably, Mary did the laundry and diapers, along with the cooking, as was customary at the time. In addition, Jesus' respect for marriage was such that He impressed upon His followers the revolutionary principle of indissolubility, declaring that "what God has joined together" let "no man put asunder." Matthew, Mark, Luke, and Paul all indicate, beyond any reasonable doubt, that Our Lord was unconditional in forbidding remarriage after divorce.[15]

Reconciliation

It hardly seems possible that mere mortals could possess the power to confer God's pardon. Yet Christ told Peter and the other apostles as a group: *"Whose sins you shall forgive, they are forgiven, and whose sins you shall retain, they are retained"* (*John* 20:23).

Confession calls for courage on the part of the penitent, but how exhilarating it is to know that one has been made clean in the eyes of God! Among non-believers, some are so enamored of reconciliation as a sacrament that they regard it as the most appealing feature of Catholicism! Psychiatrists, too, have long recognized its utility as a means of removing guilt; indeed, it is curious that people will pay for the privilege of reclining on a doctor's couch when they can go to Confession free of charge. Perhaps they stay away from the confessional because they know the priest will echo Christ's charge to the woman caught in adultery: *"Go and sin no more."* Yet this is precisely what they are most in need of hearing. Just as an automobile requires periodic oil changes to lubricate its moving parts and improve performance, so, too, in the case of the soul. We need to have our "spiritual fluids" refreshed from time to time if we are to avoid a build-up of the kind of moral sludge that erodes the joy of conscious integrity and hampers our relations with others.

There should be ample opportunity for Confession at neighborhood churches. But in an emergency, anyone can walk into any Catholic rectory at any time, ask for a priest, and normally he will be happy to oblige.

---

15. See appendix B.

Hell

It is not fashionable in today's topsy-turvy world to dwell on the torments of Hell. But the truth of the matter is that damnation is mentioned dozens of times in the Bible. Christ Himself described it as "everlasting fire" where there would be "the weeping and gnashing of teeth," a phrase that appears no less than four times in the Gospel of Matthew alone.

The point to bear in mind is that there are two kinds of sin: mortal and venial. Mortal sin, the more serious of the two, bars us from Holy Communion and consigns us to Hell unless we go to Confession or make a perfect Act of Contrition on our deathbed. However, in order for a sin to be mortal, it has to meet three criteria:

1. It must be a serious matter.
2. We must be aware of its seriousness.
3. We must act with full consent of the will—
   that is to say, we must know exactly what
   we are doing, be fully aware of the consequences, and act with full deliberation.

If any one of these conditions is absent, the sin in question is venial, and we are not *obliged* to confess it. One hastens to add, however, that even venial sin is an affront to God, and, as such, *we are urged not to take such offenses lightly.* All too often, when we don't aim at perfection as Christ recommended *("Be ye perfect even as your Heavenly Father is perfect"),* we find ourselves sliding in the opposite direction.

One or two examples will suffice to illustrate the difference between venial and mortal sin. Let us assume, for the sake of argument, that we are with friends and the talk turns suggestive or verges on malicious gossip. We are taken by surprise, and before we know it, an off-color joke has drawn laughs or someone's reputation has been dragged through the mud. We may feel mean for not having tried to change the the subject, but we have not sinned mortally because the thing we did, or failed to do, was unintentional. If, on the other hand, we and our partner have chosen to live together as man and wife before marriage; if, in addition, we realize that the Church views such conduct as a serious offense against God; and if, finally, in spite of knowing that the Church enjoins us to call a halt, see a priest, confess, and carry out the prescribed penance, we insist on going our way, we are in a state of mortal sin.

As a rule, we are apt to find one sin particularly hard to root out, and this can be discouraging. Returning again and again to the confessional with the same old story can seem pointless, if not self-defeating. Yet isn't this what one does on the physical level to fight disease? Do we not take antibiotic pills over and over again? Does a cancer patient not submit to repeated radiation as part of chemotherapy? If we were to go after moral cancer with the same kind of determination, could we not expect similar results? Interior change takes time, but God will not deny us the power we need if we ask for it often enough and indicate at each step along the way a renewed willingness to do our part. Christ came on earth to conquer sin, and He will give us the grace we need to conquer ourselves if we receive the Sacrament of Penance with a firm purpose of amendment, coupled with a practical plan of reform.

Here again, there is a direct application to the married state, for to seek reconciliation with God by facing our shortcomings and doing so regularly, say at least once a month, is to cultivate humility, and it is this virtue, more than any other, which will enable us to remain cheerful in moments of distress and yield on matters of personal preference.

Communion

A good confession is like a good shower after days of personal neglect. It spruces us up and paves the way for a worthy reception of Holy Communion, the third of the spiritual resources recommended for couples seeking to keep their love alive and fresh. Those who receive Our Lord's Body and Blood avail themselves of the greatest privilege known to man, something so mystical and awesome that it caused many of Christ's disciples to break with Him because they could not believe He was serious when He said, *"Unless you eat the flesh of the Son of Man and drink His blood you shall not have life in you...* [for] *my flesh is food indeed, and my blood is drink indeed."* Note that Jesus insisted on a literal interpretation of these words when He let the malcontents go rather than offer further explanation (*John* 6:54-57).

Our Lord knew something that we humans have a tendency to forget: namely, that the soul needs sustenance as much as the body if it is to retain a sense of well-being, and the Eucharist is the most nourishing of all foods. There have always been those who claim that it is sufficient for them to pray at home and perform good works. What about regular church-goers, they ask, who are anything but God fearing on the other six days of the week? Appearances can be deceptive, however. Statistics indicate that those who attend church regularly are more than twice as likely to remain married as their stay-at-home brethren. They are also apt to live longer, have fewer heart attacks, and experience a lower incidence of hypertension, arteriosclerosis, and high blood pressure. Equally to the point, a 1990 Gallup poll indicates that they give four times as much to charity and volunteer twice as much of their time. They are nearly twice as likely to donate to non-religious charities, and if one credits the *New York Times,* they are much less likely to cheat on their income tax.[16]

With a certain amount of preparation beforehand and a sincere act of thanksgiving afterward, reception of Christ's Body and Blood helps us subdue our carnal appetites. This is important because, contrary to the popular impression, marriage does not shield us from temptation. Whether single or married, we must strive resolutely to drive out impure thoughts and exercise self-control.

Fasting and Abstinence

One of the best methods of staying spiritually fit, as well as preparing for Communion, is to fast and abstain from choice foods as a symbol of the sorrow that we feel, or *ought* to feel, for our many sins.[17] Such a practice used to be mandatory on Fridays. Today, one is permitted to substitute some other kind of mortification. But there is still plenty of room for the method recommended by Jesus, Peter, John, and Paul (*Matt.* 6:17-18, 9:14-15; *1 Peter* 2:11; *1 Cor.* 9:27). Just as it is wise, when one drives an automobile on ice, to apply the brakes every so often just to make sure one is in control, so, too, when it comes to the "braking" of the body. Life is slippery and the body treacherous. We want to be sure we are in control in times of temptation. Fasting is also the road to humility. It reminds us of who we are and Whom we serve, just as it reinforces our willingness to sacrifice when our lives are difficult. A family that goes without dessert on Friday is also in a position to donate the

---

16. *New York Times,* 20 April 1991, p. 10; Philip Yancey, "God is Good for You," *Catholic Digest* (February 1992), pp. 1-2; *National Catholic Register,* 24 May 1992, p. 5. See also appendix D.
17. According to the new *Catechism,* "There is no holiness without renunciation and spiritual battle" (section 2015).

amount of their saving to church on Sunday, thus enhancing the benefit to all.

APOSTOLIC ZEAL

Thus far, we have focused on the effect of deepening religious commitment on conjugal relations. True spirituality, however, operates on an extremely broad front, reaching out to friends, relatives, neighbors, and the world at large in accord with Jesus' command: *"If you did it to the least of my brethren, you did it to me"* (*Matt.* 25:40). As in the game of tennis, if you don't serve, you can't win. We may be too busy to chauffeur a handicapped person to church or to babysit for someone who might otherwise have to miss Sunday Mass. Perhaps we find ourselves under too much pressure to lector, teach catechism, or help the pastor with a paint job. Will we then have a stack of postcards handy to contact the sponsors of TV programs, indicating support or voicing concern as the case may be?

In other words, what form will our charity take? Are we prepared to speak out on such issues as abortion and premarital sex? Have we studied controversial topics in the light of Church teaching? Are we ready to support couples whose matrimonial bonds show signs of snapping, telling them, when they come to us in trouble, that we will gladly help them put their marriages back together again, but we won't help tear them apart?

Our work itself can be tremendously fruitful as a means of sanctification, not only for ourselves but for those around us, if we do it cheerfully, labor to the best of our ability, and provided also we are prepared to take risks. A lawyer friend of mine once remarked that when clients came to him for advice about initiating divorce proceedings, he would do all he could to save the marriage, even if it meant a loss of income. Accountants who refuse to engage in deliberate falsification of figures may find themselves in the same situation. There is a price to be paid for following the path of virtue. But from a spiritual point of view, any losses we may incur are greatly outweighed by the gains.

Spirituality, like sunshine, casts its rays in every direction and over all sectors of life, whether they be professional, domestic, or recreational. Take something as mundane as a family trip. It will be more rewarding if, in addition to the usual tourist attractions, one takes in some sites of religious significance. Obviously, you will stop in Paris if you visit France. But those who go out of their way to include Lourdes on the itinerary will be deeply touched by the contact they make with a truly compelling story of faith. Just as one would target the Holy Land on a trip to the Middle East, or the Vatican if one's destination were Italy, how could one tour Portugal without making a pilgrimage to Fatima, site of the most spectacular and most thoroughly authenticated of all miracles? In our own hemisphere, on the outskirts of Mexico City, we are fortunate to have the Shrine of Our Lady of Guadalupe. As at Lourdes and Fatima, visitors to Guadalupe will be profoundly moved by their proximity to a miracle that is once again overwhelming. And what if you are planning a trip closer to home? There will be Catholic churches along the way, some of them attractive, some of them less so, but all of them houses of God. So why not drop in, from time to time, and spend a moment before the tabernacle to keep that conversation with Jesus going? What could be more refreshing?

I realize that the above recommendations may sound like a tall order, especially when all of them are lumped together. But remember, they are merely suggestions. The only mistake one can make that is really serious in connection with spirituality is to underrate its importance.

WHEN YOU PRAY

One last thought about prayer: when you lift up your voice to Heaven, don't expect God to return a booming response. At times, the silence from on high can be almost deafening! But keep on praying. He will answer in one form or another, even if it takes time. And if His answer turns out to be "No," you can be sure that, like any other responsible parent, He has His reasons. His message may come in the form of a coincidence that sets us thinking or even in the guise of trials and tribulations that open new vistas.

How would you react if you found that you could not have all the children you wanted? Would it surprise you if this were God's way of intimating that He had something else in mind for you, something different but just as worthwhile? Perhaps He wants you to spend a portion of your time ministering to the needs of other families. Assuming your spouse is agreeable, you might opt for adoption or devote yourself more fully to your work. The point is that if we "look and listen" when confronted with life's roadblocks, we may find that what at first appeared to be an obstacle in our path is actually a friendly sign pointing us in the direction we need to go.[18]

IN SUM

There was a time when Catholics as a whole were more resistant than other groups to marital breakdown. No longer. Remarriage after divorce may be less prevalent among Catholics than it is among non-Catholics, but the rate of first-time failure is about the same. By and large, the members of our Church are not as interested as they once were in the extraordinary sources of strength that

---

18. The new *Catechism* makes it clear that children are not something owed to a couple by God, but rather a gift (sec. 2378).

an extraordinary faith has to offer. They think they are serious about making their marriage work, but how serious can they be when they go on ignoring the critical dimension of spirituality? How serious can they be if they are not interested in learning more about their faith and practicing it with sufficient fervor to sail in perfect calmness over a very troubled sea? If only they knew that God stands ready at all times to change the water of their ordinary everyday existence into the fine wine of life-long love and devotion!

Over a thousand years ago, a wise monk named Benedict condensed almost all of this into a single paragraph, one that is worth committing to memory:

> There is a good zeal that can lead a married couple to God and to everlasting life. Practice this zeal, then, with most fervent love. Be the first to show respect. Support with patience one another's weaknesses, whether they be of body or of character. Compete with one another in showing mutual obedience. Do what you consider useful for each other rather than what is useful for yourself. Love one another with sincere affection, and have a loving fear of God. Prefer nothing whatever to Christ.

Part 5

Catholic Sexual Ethics

We have reserved our discussion of the physiological side of marriage until now because physical gratification is not only less important than other elements of the marital picture (such as good communication and a healthy relationship with God); it *presupposes* them. Although much fuss is made by so-called "experts" about what happens, or fails to happen, in the bedroom, such talk may be taken with a grain of salt. In a good many instances, sex has been oversold.

This is not to deny that love-making is a good thing, indeed a glorious thing. Despite what critics say, the Catholic Church does not regard the body as a necessary evil. Isolated figures within the Church may have expressed themselves in this way on occasion, but not the Church as a whole. On the contrary, it has defended the procreative act as something distinctly positive and holy. Granted, the Holy See hews to its teaching that, of all human appetites, the sexual drive is unique in the degree to which it must be brought under control if it is to be man's servant rather than his master. And this is so because marital intercourse, unlike eating and drinking, is potentially life-giving and, therefore, attended with consequences calling for a mature exercise of responsibility. Nevertheless, there is nothing here to suggest inhibition.

The Church is not so much "puritanical" as simply concerned—and with good reason. Owing to the lofty purpose for which the marital act was intended, sexual license amounts to a form of sacrilege, and the manifold abuses to which it leads have been roundly condemned: fornication (premarital sex), adultery (extra-marital affairs), masturbation (private or between spouses), incest, homosexuality (when active), bestiality, artificial contraception, and pornography, to name a few.[19] Lust of any kind is enormously destructive since it strikes at the very core of a person and, as such, throws his or her entire life, along with that of others, into disarray.

SEX IS ABOUT BABIES

God engineered human life in such a way that physical interaction between man and woman would result in new life. In addition, Adam and Eve were specifically *commanded* to multiply (*Gen.* 1:28), just as they were warned, after committing original sin, that childbirth would be painful and that they would have to live by the sweat of their brow. Remarkably little has changed over the years. Ten to fifteen percent of all couples find that they are unable to conceive, and among the remainder there are intrinsic factors that in most cases militate against a steady stream of children arriving at nine- to twelve-month intervals. Nevertheless, one may be fairly certain of a pro-life mentality in Heaven judging from the nature of the sexual appetite and the length of the child-bearing period in a woman's life.

The Catholic idea of procreation, which is founded on natural law in consonance with God's sovereign majesty and Mary's magnificent response to the angel Gabriel, is that all children are a gift from God, whether they be

---

19. See appendix B quotations. According to the new *Catechism,* sections 1755 and 2352-53, fornication is "always wrong" and "gravely contrary to the dignity of persons," while masturbation is "an intrinsically and gravely disordered action."

many in number or few, and one must not place artificial constraints on God's generosity. Every marital act must remain open to the transmission of life.[20]

Many who defend contraception in the form of condoms, the pill, and sterilization do so on the ground that its practitioners have a worthy end in view. But such reasoning violates a cardinal tenet of the moral law: namely that one may never commit an intrinsically evil act, in this case frustration of God's will and the natural law, in order to do good. One may not steal, for instance, in order to put a needy child through college. If and when the marriage act is performed, it must be performed in its full integrity so that the gift of self is complete, and it is only complete when its procreative, as well as its unitive, function remains intact. Only when both parties are consciously prepared to give themselves totally to one another can they attain the stature to which they have been called by God.[21]

Is there not logic in the Church's belief that as products of divine engineering we should be governed by divine rules? We may think that a second, third, or fourth child has no place in our lives because the rest of the family would be denied certain benefits. Yet, this is not the way God sees it. From time immemorial, He has sent the tenderest of babes into war zones, droughts, floods, epidemics, and famines. Why? Does the Parent of parents play favorites? Or is it because pain and sacrifice, when accepted in a spirit of steadfast faith and loyalty, can

---

20. The new *Catechism,* section 2366. *The Catechism* goes on to say that "Sacred Scripture and the Church's traditional practice see in large families a sign of God's blessing and the parents' generosity" (2373).
21. The new universal *Catechism,* sections 2366-67. In the words of Pope John Paul II, in his *Letter to Families* (1994), the "total gift of self to the other involves a potential openness to procreation" (sec. 12).

unleash great redemptive power?

In times past, a large family was viewed as a blessing, and if it entailed more than the usual amount of sacrifice, this was taken in stride, for the most part, and accepted as part of the divine plan. Interestingly enough, it is only in recent years, beginning with the decade of the 1960s, that Church officials have come under mounting pressure to endorse artificial birth control, for reasons with which we are all familiar. The rate of infant mortality is falling even as life-expectancy for adults continues to rise. More and more people have gravitated to urban areas where recreational space is limited. Employees are frequently required to travel far from home, urban housing units are often cramped and small, and the only recognition accorded the ideal of family life is a meager tax deduction for dependents. Many more women are working outside the home at a time when artificial contraception is perceived by many as a safe and reliable method of family planning. Finally, from a more general standpoint, history indicates that a nation's moral fiber may be eroded by prolonged intervals of peace and prosperity.

Just as striking, though, as the direction history seems to be taking is the fact that the Catholic Church, *as a church,* has adhered so firmly to its traditional teaching on contraception. Confirmed by Pope Paul VI in his encyclical, *Humanae Vitae,* and soon thereafter by the American bishops' pastoral, *To Live in Jesus Christ* (1976), it was reaffirmed by a synod of bishops held in Rome in 1980 and repeated many times over by Pope John Paul II, notably in his *Familiaris Consortio.* Dissident theologians who suggest that traditional teaching must change with changing times have not reckoned with the Rock of Peter. Over a span of 2,000 years, no pope has ever had to retract a single position that he or one of his predecessors set forth in the realm of faith and morals—something of a miracle since there have been some popes whose personal lives were far from edifying.[22]

Granted, the Church has altered its requirements on fasting and abstinence, along with mixed marriage. Meat may now be eaten on Friday if some other way can be found of observing the spirit of the day on which Our Lord suffered and died. Likewise, in a mixed marriage, the Catholic party is no longer required to promise in writing that he or she will do everything possible to raise the children as Catholics. Such promises may be made orally. But there is a difference between disciplinary matters subject to administrative fiat and the great body of doctrine known as dogma. Basically, it comes down to a question of essentials versus non-essentials and the notion that some things will always be wrong. Rome, for example, will *never* approve of murder, suicide, fornication, or adultery.

EVERY CHILD IS A GIFT FROM GOD

The celebrated author and convert to Catholicism, G. K. Chesterton, once quipped that birth control, referring to contraceptive methods, meant "no birth and no control." Whether one is amused or annoyed by the witticism will depend upon one's spiritual orientation, what one thinks of the act designed by God to transmit human life, and what value one places on the soul that is being preconceptually aborted.

In this modern, mechanized age of ours, youngsters may appear to be less of an asset than they once were, especially for families struggling to make ends meet. This, however, does not diminish the value of such children, each of whom comes out of God's workshop with an immortal soul capable of giving great glory to its Creator. We all have an instinctive fear of deprivation—it goes

---

22. See appendix A.

with the territory. Yet when we reach deep down in our
hearts, we also realize that we do not live by bread alone.
As Christians, we have the example of our Redeemer,
Who identified with the underprivileged by living a life
of poverty and Who taught that the poor are specially
"blessed."

Adversity and hard times are not what one generally
prays for; but the record of history along with our own
experience tell us that there is no situation in life that
cannot lead to greatness. If one were to eliminate all those
born into families of ten children or more, we would have
to do without Thomas Jefferson, James Madison, Daniel
Webster, Harriet Beecher Stowe, St. Rose of Lima,
Washington Irving, Franz Schubert, St. Ignatius (last of
thirteen), John Marshall (greatest of all U. S. chief justices
and one of fifteen children), Benjamin Franklin (one of
seventeen), Enrico Caruso (eighteenth in a family of
twenty-one), and Catherine of Siena (twenty-fourth of
twenty-five). The roster of men and women who lost one
or both parents at an early age contains still another
honor roll. Robert E. Lee, one of the most gifted Civil War
generals, was only five when his father walked out of his
life, never to return. Prize-winning Russian novelist Alexander Solzhenitsyn never knew his father, and Confucius
of China was an orphan from practically the day he was
born.[23]

Obviously, no one is obliged to go out of his or her
way to have a large family, even though sociologists tell
us that such families tend to be closely knit with parents
who are confident, accomplished, and devoted. Nor is
anyone obligated to have recourse to a fertility clinic
where procedures can be as frustrating as they are
intrusive.

On the other hand, based on our belief that God loves

---

23. For other examples, see appendix J.

all His children equally and that He is not in the business of making mistakes, there is only one logical conclusion to be drawn. As soon as one begins to impugn His generosity by assuming that a child born in affluence is a gift, as compared with one born in difficult circumstances (presumably a curse), one ceases to be Christian in the fullest sense of the word.

THE MYTH OF OVERPOPULATION

How easy it is to succumb to the notion of "people as pollution." Today's media is full of references to "overpopulation," as if our towns and cities were so many tree nurseries or game preserves, as if our children were nothing but costly and time-consuming, a risk to the mother's figure and a barrier to intimacy. The mother in St. Louis who bears a fourth or fifth child is supposed to feel guilty for adding to the burden of Calcutta! Even in Calcutta, we know that life among the poorest of the poor is far from insupportable.

Virtually every prediction by population doomsayers since the time of Parson Malthus (1766-1834) has proven false. One of the more recent examples is Paul Ehrlich's *Population Explosion*, published in 1968 and since discredited. A later work, *The Population Bomb*, shows no sign of being any more reliable. No nation, least of all the United States, is running out of land. Ninety-seven percent of America remains undeveloped, with towns, cities, railroads, and airports occupying a mere three percent. There is no real connection, either, between population density worldwide and what we call poverty. In the Far East, the most crowded nations are actually the ones that enjoy the highest standard of living—Japan, Taiwan, and Singapore, for example. The population of East Germany under Communist rule was less than that of West Germany. Yet, its standard of living sagged terribly under an alien political-economic system.

Clearly, poverty has more to do with government policy than with procreation. According to Jacqueline Kasun, professor of economics at California State University, world agricultural resources could support 22 times as many people using our present methods of farming. Africa alone could feed twice the current world population. The hunger that does exist affects only about two percent of the world's people, and it is generally related to civil war, as in Somalia, or hardline Marxist agricultural policies coupled with ineffective distribution.[24]

Different holy fathers have said the same thing over and over again in different ways: namely, that the answer to population pressure is not to turn people away from the table but rather to furnish more food while making it possible for one parent to remain at home. On the latter point, Holy Father John Paul II cautions that:

> Society must be structured in such a way that wives and mothers are not compelled to work outside the home and that their families can live and prosper in a dignified way even when they themselves devote their full time to their own family (*Familiaris Consortio,* 23).

One would never know from much of the talk one hears that children have a supernatural birthright, that each one of them comes into the world with a ready-made passport to Heaven. Surely, it is one of today's best-kept secrets that all of God's sons and daughters, whether rich or poor, educated or uneducated, are in full possession of the legacy that such a paternity implies. As Scripture has it, *"Let the little ones come to me. . . seek first the kingdom of God and all things will be added unto you"* (*Matt.* 6:33 and 19:13-15).

---

24. *National Catholic Register,* January 3, 1993, p. 5. For more on the myth of overpopulation, see appendix I.

This, of course, is the spiritual side of the equation. But it is vital. Without wishing to lose sight of the fact that health, housing, and education are undeniable needs, and costly ones as well, we must never forget that man is more than flesh and blood; he is primarily spiritual in nature, and it is his spiritual impulses that cry out the loudest for expression. Living one's life in accord with God's commandments is not always easy. But it is essential that we guard against allowing material considerations to override the supernatural imperative which permeates our inmost being and provides the key to our destiny.

We hear much nowadays about "quality of life." Note carefully how the word "quality" is defined: in such a way that immortal souls created by God for His greater glory count for nothing unless they are well provided for here on earth. Can't you just hear Satan chortling?

The irony is that suicide rates, always a telling indicator of desperation, happen to be highest among the rich. Have you ever stopped to ask yourself why, among permanently crippled paraplegics, the suicide rate is practically zero? Or why, in God's scheme of things, happiness turns up in the most unexpected places? Why is it that facial expressions among inhabitants of the least affluent nations are every bit as bright, perhaps brighter, than those of America's favored rich? Pay a visit some day to one of the "less fortunate" countries of our hemisphere, and you will find crime rates disproportionately low. Pope John Paul II pointed out that our society is "awash in consumerism," and the more one ponders his words, the more one realizes that generosity in procreation is not only a sign of our love; it is also a clear witness to the trust we place in Divine Providence. Is there a price to be paid? Yes. But the same may be said for any worthwhile endeavor.

A SENSE OF PIETY

Most of us would agree that there are certain things in life that one will refrain from doing simply as a matter of form. If an older child sucks his thumb in public, Mom and Dad can disapprove without having to adduce fifty-nine reasons. Likewise, if a person comes to Sunday Mass clad in an undershirt and bathing trunks, the priest has a perfect right to object without furnishing arguments capable of overwhelming the intellect of an Einstein. Just as there is a social sense that adds up to good manners, so too there is a spiritual sense that translates into a profound reverence for human life. If socially disadvantaged children are apt to grow up without a sense of propriety, youngsters who are spiritually deprived, however affluent and well-mannered, are likely to mature without a sense of piety. The point is that those who are truly refined in spirit will sense instinctively that there is "something wrong" with artificial contraception, not to mention *in vitro* fertilization, artificial insemination, and genetic engineering.[25] And if they don't have such a sense, they will at least entertain arguments to this effect.

It should be noted, in addition, that the logic behind

---

25. See the new *Catechism,* sections 2376-78: "Techniques that entail the dissociation of husband and wife by the intrusion of a person other than the couple (donation of sperm or ovum, surrogate uterus) are gravely immoral." Techniques involving only the married couple (artificial insemination and fertilization) are "perhaps less reprehensible, yet remain morally unacceptable." They dissociate the sexual act from the procreative act, and thus entrust "the life and identity of the embryo into the power of doctors and biologists" which, in turn, "establishes the domination of technology over the origin and destiny of the human person...contrary to the dignity and equality that must be common to parents and children." All of this is, of course, in line with the idea that children are a gift from God rather than something owed (2378).

contraception can be used to justify masturbation, abortion, mercy killing, and suicide.

Skeptics will argue that frustration of the procreative process is no different morally from the use of earplugs to shut out unwanted noise. But such a comparison does not stand up under close scrutiny. Hearing may be wonderful, but it is not sacred in the sense that it involves the conception of a human soul destined to live forever. Nor does it entail the same kind of direct intervention by God.

NATURAL FAMILY PLANNING

Let it be said in this connection that the Church has always sanctioned periodic abstinence from marital intercourse for "grave" reasons (*Humanae Vitae,* n. 10). Such reasons could be economic, social, psychological, or medical, such as a serious threat to the life of the mother or child. In years past, the name given to such a practice was "rhythm." Today, however, there is a new Church-approved method called Natural Family Planning (NFP) which, as a means of postponing pregnancy or avoiding it altogether, is more scientific than rhythm. By enabling a couple to identify the fertile period of a woman's monthly cycle with a high degree of accuracy, approximately 98 percent of the time, NFP has been adopted by non-Catholics, as well as Catholics, owing to the absence of hazardous side effects.[26]

Cynics, who regard NFP as an inferior form of birth control because it requires abstinence for a week to ten days during the prime time of a woman's cycle, empha-

---

26. The 98-99 percent success rate of NFP, assuming it is properly practiced, contrasts quite favorably with that of the pill (93-95 percent), condoms, diaphrams, and cervical caps (94 percent), and spermicides (74 percent). See *Time,* 26 February 1990, p. 44, for failure rates; also *Twin Circle,* 16 February 1992, p. 19.

size the element of risk and argue that it must be backed up by abortion. Such views are understandable, but they oversimplify a highly complex issue.

NFP, to begin with, is not just birth control by another name. It differs substantially from artificial contraception in that it neither frustrates the procreative process directly nor impairs the integrity of sexual intercourse. To put it another way, NFP does not sever the unity between love and life that God so obviously intended for the procreative act; separation of the biological from the procreative aspect of sex puts masturbation in the same category as artificial contraception. But apart from the moral issue, the mere fact that NFP entails sacrifice and some degree of risk can lead to a heightening of mutual respect between partners as well as to increased satisfaction during "safe" periods. It is also less likely than artificial contraception to arouse suspicion on the part of the husband and become a bone of contention between man and wife during the springtime of their union.[27]

There are only two caveats, assuming both parties are willing to practice NFP and it does not become an occasion of sin, especially the sin of incontinence.[28] The first of these is the fact that NFP, to be effective, presupposes some degree of intelligence, coupled with a considerable amount of self-control. Rare is the husband and wife team that can claim total self-possession at all times. Human nature being what it is, there is bound to be a factor of uncertainty. Three out of ten men surveyed in a 1989 nationwide poll conducted by the Diocesan Development

---

27. Imagine, for example, a husband who wants a child desperately. His wife has been on the pill for some time, but she gladly agrees to stop. He is by nature suspicious, and she does not conceive. Knowing that she is not opposed to contraception in principle, he might suspect her of using it surreptitiously, despite all of her assurances to the contrary.

28. Rev. Herbert Jone, O.F.M., *Moral Theology* (Rockford, Illinois: TAN Books & Publishers, 1991), p. 542.

Program for Natural Family Planning, said they were dissatisfied with NFP's performance in avoiding pregnancy.[29] It thus seems fair to say that if "grave reasons" were not mandated in order to justify NFP on moral grounds, they would be necessary in a good many cases for the system itself to work. And even here, there is no substitute for total abstinence if the situation involves something as serious as the life of the mother or well-being of a potential child.

The other caveat is that NFP is not permissible for all couples under all circumstances, only for those with "grave reasons" for limiting the size of their family. As to what constitutes "grave reasons," it is hard to speak categorically. Such matters are best resolved in conference with a spiritual director whose judgment one trusts —and trusts not because it is lenient, but rather because it squares with the teaching of the Magisterium. The yearning for a more attractive home or one situated in a more desirable neighborhood would certainly not qualify. Neither would the desire to take a longer vacation or to send one's children to prestigious schools.

Church teaching on artificial contraception is undeniably tough. Oftentimes, it requires sacrifice, even heroic sacrifice. But this is equally true of the Church's position on indissolubility of marriage, premarital sex, and homosexuality. Life itself is tough. Nothing worthwhile has ever been accomplished without blood, sweat, and tears. How remarkable that even in our so-called modern age, childbirth is nearly always attended by danger and anxiety. Difficulty alone does not automatically disqualify a course of action or invalidate a teaching. If, on the human level, parental discipline, conjoined with affection, conduces to the long-range happiness and well-being of the child, is it not reasonable to view God as

---

29. *Our Sunday Visitor,* 17 May 1992, p. 5.

a demanding parent whose children benefit from the divine discipline?

Catholic doctrine is beautifully in keeping with the whole concept of sex as something sacred, something in which God is uniquely and intimately involved. How can one profess to believe in God and God's fatherhood ("Our Father, Who art in Heaven...") and not have great respect for every act linked with such parenthood? Often, one will hear it said that "I couldn't possibly afford another pregnancy," or, "My wife would go insane with another child...already we lack sufficient space, privacy, and material comfort." The answer to these objections is that God never gives any of us more than we can bear, and bear profitably. Parents of large families will tell you they didn't know how they could ever manage with a third or fourth child until the child in question actually arrived, and...they managed! One is reminded of the old Spanish proverb: "Every child comes with its own loaf of bread under its arm."

When all is said and done, there is nothing the world of today needs so much as a counter-cultural faith that relies on God's grace and recognizes an authority in the realm of morals that is insulated from politics, popularity contests, and conventional views—an authority backed by God's Holy Spirit that boasts a record of undeviating adherence to the truth for over 2,000 years.

MARITAL INTERCOURSE

The worst thing that can happen to sex—the surest way to ruin it, in fact—is to place too much of a premium on it. As indicated above, the physical side of love-making cannot stand alone. It is unique in its absolute dependence on the proper functioning of other elements. Thus, if husband and wife are psychologically at odds, they are unlikely to find what they are looking for in the marriage bed—not for any length of time, at least.

How often couples should engage in intercourse depends entirely on the situation. Three times a day or three times a year can both be "right," depending on such factors as health, pregnancy, and the pressure of work. No spouse wants to be regarded as an automaton. Besides, true joy tends to catch us unawares at moments we least expect and at times when we are least self-conscious.

Beware of preconceived notions of "compatibility." Sexual gratification often lags behind desire. One or the other partner, or both, may be tired, nervous, or distracted, and such a condition can obtain for protracted lengths of time. At times like this, one's aim should be to express love and tenderness in whatever way is possible. The irony is that the more one forgets about self and concentrates on the "other," the greater the sense of personal fulfillment. Jesus held that to "save" one's life, one must "lose" it, and there is no better example of this, perhaps, than in the mystical relationship we call marriage.

Husbands generally take the lead in love-making. But again, there are no hard and fast rules except to say that a considerate partner will not make advances when the other is plainly exhausted or, for any other reason, seriously indisposed. In addition, neither partner should discourage sexual advances without sufficient cause and without assuring his or her mate that intimacy is only a matter of time. One would not want one's mate to feel discouraged or to "give up," so to speak. As St. Paul put it,

> *Let the husband render to the wife her due, and likewise the wife to the husband. The wife has not authority over her body, but the husband; the husband likewise has not authority over his body, but the wife. Do not deprive each other, except perhaps by consent, for a time, that you may give yourselves to prayer; and*

> *return together again lest Satan tempt you*
> *because you lack self-control* (*1 Cor.* 7:3-6).

Naturally, there will be times when one may have to forego union in order to attend to the duties of a well-ordered life. It would be imprudent on a regular basis, for instance, to put one's love life ahead of professional or family responsibilities, not to mention one's obligation to God.

It goes without saying, too, that no one is ever obliged to engage in love-making that is indecent. Anything that might be offensive to a spirit of moderation, modesty, and refinement is out of the question. One's spouse may never be regarded as the object of lustful desire (*Gaudium et Spes,* No. 51). But having said this, one can be as passionate and uninhibited as one likes as long as both parties feel comfortable and retain their dignity as children of God (*1 Thess.* 4:3-5).

One or two other observations will suffice. It is not a good practice to give the impression of desiring physical intimacy unless one is actually prepared to follow through. To lead one's mate on, as it were, would be just as wrong as foisting one's passion on an unsuspecting partner without laying the proper groundwork. Tokens of affection tendered in the hours and days preceding sexual union, as well as a gradual lead-up to the act itself, can be of great importance, particularly to the woman. Finally, there is a need for both parties to pace themselves so that the "faster" one, usually the man, allows the one who is "slower" to catch up. He must exercise control while she strives to "let go" so as to compensate for a slower pace of arousal.

WHY LISTEN TO THE CHURCH?

Some of my readers may wonder why something as natural as love-making should be hedged about with so many rules and regulations. The answer is simple: this is the way God made it. There is a divine instruction manual for every human activity, and it is worth consulting. Most of the rules are self-evident, and for the rest we can rely on Peter and his successors. All of which brings us full circle to the need for discipline and papal teaching. Anyone who is tempted to doubt the authority of the Catholic Church because it makes greater demands than other churches, should remember that Christ Himself took an extremely hard line on many questions. Time and again, He held His disciples to a standard of behavior that can only be described as exacting. Was it not normal for the twelve to be terrified when they were rocked by a storm on the Sea of Galilee? Yet Jesus rebuked them for their lack of trust, exclaiming, *"O you of little faith!"* When Peter suggested that the Messiah needn't suffer at the hands of His enemies—a human enough sentiment— Our Lord recoiled angrily, calling him "Satan" and bidding him *"get behind me!"* (*Mark* 8:33).

Christ's teaching on marriage was so rigid by the standards of the day that it caused His apostles to inquire, "Who, then, should get married?" At which point, instead of qualifying what He had to say, He went a step further and stated a preference for celibacy (*Matt.* 19:10-12). Again, when one of His followers, who had expressed interest in the ministry, pleaded for permission to attend the funeral of his father before joining the apostolate, the Master would not hear of it: *"Leave the dead to bury the dead,"* was His reply. When another would-be follower asked if he could return home and bid his family farewell before signing on, this too was denied. *"No one,"* returned Jesus, *"having put his hand to the plough and looking back, is worthy of the kingdom of God"* (*Luke* 9:59-62).

Our Lord may have been kind and compassionate when dealing with repentant sinners, but He was not easy. The adulteress who escaped death by stoning, owing to His timely intervention, found herself under a firm injunction to *"Go and sin no more!"* This was an individual who taught that it was sinful even to look at a woman with lust, let alone commit adultery. Here was a Savior who warned that the gate to His kingdom was "narrow" and that "few" would enter (*Matt.* 7:13-14). Jesus denounced whole classes of people—lawyers, scribes, and Pharisees. He cautioned against riches, declared the poor "blessed," and subjected certain towns to scorching condemnation, among them Capharnaum (His headquarters), Corozain, and Bethsaida (home to three of His apostles). Now if Our Lord was so unbending and stern in ways that ran against the grain, and which still do, would He not want His Church to reflect something of this same quality down through the years? From all that we know about life as an endurance test, what reason do we have to expect that eternal happiness can be purchased on the cheap? Just as the ways of God are not the ways of man, neither should one expect the ways of God's holy Church to be the ways of man.

Those who doubt that Christ established a religious organization with genuine authority to bind in matters of faith and morals should consult Sacred Scripture. Hundreds, if not thousands, of first-generation Christians gave their lives for the privilege of testifying to the truth of what this Scripture contains. And they did it within 30 to 40 years of Jesus' crucifixion. Many of them were eyewitnesses of Christ's ministry or, at the very least, acquainted with persons who had walked and talked with Our Lord. Yet none of them, as far as we know, had any difficulty accepting the Resurrection. None denied the existence of an organization divinely vested with power and authority. Christ Himself designated 72 disciples (*Luke* 10:1) and above them in rank twelve apostles. For the principal position of authority, He chose Peter, and it was to Peter alone that He entrusted the "keys to the kingdom of Heaven," to Peter alone that He gave the instruction: *"Feed my lambs, feed my sheep"* (see appendix A).

THE ROLE OF CONSCIENCE

One reason why it is absolutely vital to accept the Holy Father as head of the Church is because individual priests, indeed even groups of bishops have been known, on occasion, to err. Recall the English bishops at the time of Henry VIII. When Henry filed for divorce from his first wife, Catherine, and sought permission to remarry, the Holy Father responded with a polite but firm refusal. And how did the bishops react? Only one of them risked the ire of the court to side with Rome. Only one joined Sir Thomas More, Henry's chancellor and the second most powerful man in the realm, in a course that led to martyrdom. It is immaterial that Henry executed two wives and married several others. The crux of the issue is that his defiance, linked with the defection of an overwhelming majority of bishops, caused most of England to separate from the Catholic Church.

Some who sided with Henry may have done so in good conscience, but this does not make them any the less wrong. Well-meaning individuals commit egregious acts every day out of sheer ignorance. One's conscience is never proof against error unless it is formed in light of what the Holy Father teaches, and we are thus obliged, when in doubt, to be unsparing in our effort to ascertain papal teaching.

Let's face it, truth and justice have never been the path to riches and fame. The Church's teachings will always appear "unrealistic" to men and women of the world, particularly so today. Ours is a society where generosity in family matters reaps few, if any, rewards. Since many of us find ourselves in a quandary, it may seem naive, if not suicidal, to embrace Catholic values. But we must not be discouraged. Christ Himself, during His public ministry, convinced relatively few of the truth of His message. Yet, there were those at the time who recognized Him as "the Way, the Truth, and the Life," just as there will always be some wise enough to see that truth does not always coincide with the view of the majority. There were not many then, nor are there many today. But those who are brave enough, and sufficiently confident in God's Providence, to sacrifice for their ideals will receive grace in abundance. Theirs will be a joy that is deep and lasting in the present world—their yoke will be easy, their burden light—and when the time comes for them to die, they will know that they have run the race and kept the course and that their Savior has prepared a special place for them in Heaven.

Part 6

Appendix A

The Case for Papal Teaching Authority

The case for papal infallibility, which assumes that a pontiff is speaking as head of the Church *(ex cathedra)* and addressing the Church as a whole on matters of faith and morals, rests to a large degree on Christ's charge to Peter:

> *Thou art Peter, and upon this rock I will build my Church and the gates of Hell shall not prevail against it. I will give thee the keys to the kingdom of Heaven, and whatever thou shalt bind on earth shall be bound in Heaven. Whatever thou shalt loose on earth shall be loosed in Heaven (Matt. 16:18-19).*

The interpretation that Peter was simply one of the twelve apostles with no special authority is at best strained. Sacred Scripture, as well as Tradition, portrays Peter as unique in many ways. Although Christ gave the power to forgive sins to the twelve as a whole *(John 20:19-23)*, it was to Peter alone that He entrusted the "keys." Peter is mentioned first in every official list of apostles *(Matt. 10:1-4; Mark 3:16-19; Luke 6:14-16; Acts 1:13)*. He is the only one Christ is known to have singled out as a special object of prayer *(Luke 22:32)* just as he is the only one whose name was changed by Jesus—from Simon to Peter (meaning "rock"). The change is significant. Peter alone received Christ's commission to *"feed my lambs, feed my sheep"* (*John* 21:15-17). He alone was instructed to *"strengthen thy brethren"* (*Luke* 22:31-32). He was also the first to be called to the priesthood, along with his brother Andrew (*Mark* 1:16-19). He was the first to identify Our Lord as the Messiah (*Mark* 8:29), and following the crucifixion, he was the first of the twelve to enter the empty tomb (*John* 20:6). Jesus made a point of asking Peter whether he loved Him more than any of the other apostles, and Peter answered in the affirmative (*John* 21:15). Peter is the only apostle known to have received Jesus into his home (*Matt.* 8:14-17).

Our Lord promised His apostles that He would send them the Paraclete, the "Spirit of Truth," and that it would teach them "all the truth" and dwell with them "forever" (*John* 14:16-17; 16:13). Later, after He ascended into Heaven, followed by His sending of the Holy Spirit to strengthen His apostles at Pentecost, it was Peter who decided on the method of choosing a new apostle to replace Judas (*Acts* 1:15-26). Subsequently, Peter was the first to preach on behalf of the Church (*Acts* 2:14), the first to take Christianity to the Gentiles (*Acts* 10), and the first to work a cure. Significantly, he was the only one of the twelve to raise a person from the dead (*Acts* 9:36-43). His power over illness and disease was such that the sick would wait patiently for his shadow to fall upon them as he passed (*Acts* 5:12-16). One might add that Peter was the only one of the twelve in whose presence a man and a woman were struck dead for chicanery (*Acts* 5:1-11). Finally, Peter was the only author of Sacred Scripture ever to pronounce judgment on another such author. In one of his letters, he says that Paul's writings are not only difficult to grasp but likely to confuse those who may be unstable in their faith or lacking in erudition (*2 Peter* 3:16).

Peter was consulted on every major issue that arose in the early Church, and in every case it was his judgment that prevailed (see, for example, *Acts* 1:15-26; 5:29;

15:6-12, and *John* 21:1-9). The same may be said of each of his successors, the bishops of Rome. True, he "peters out" in the second half of *Acts,* but the second half is less about Church administration than about Paul's mission to the Gentiles.

Peter established himself at the seat of empire from whence the Church was able to reach out to the rest of the world. One might add that every major nation ever converted to Christianity received the faith from missionaries who were either commissioned by or in communion with Peter and his successors. Then, too, all the ecumenical councils ever held, beginning with the Council of Nicaea in 325 A.D., were either convened by the bishop of Rome or approved by him.

Recently, the Second Vatican Council made it clear in decrees promulgated by Pope Paul VI (21 December 1964) that:

> The Pope's power of primacy over all remains whole and intact. In virtue of his office, the Roman Pontiff has full, supreme, and universal power over the Church, which he is always free to exercise...infallibility also resides in the body of bishops, but only when it exercises the supreme teaching authority *with* the Pope.*

The Council also stated in its *Dogmatic Constitution on the Church* that:

> Religious submission of mind and will must be shown in a special way to the authentic teaching authority of the Roman Pontiff, even when he is not speaking ex-Cathedra (*Lumen Gentium,* sec. 25).

---

* Quotations are taken from an outline of Council documents published by the bishop of Rockville Centre (New York) in 1965, pp. 11-12, 15, 86.

Significantly, no pope has ever endorsed any kind of heresy or proclaimed anything in the realm of faith or morals which has had to be retracted. Pope Liberius, whose tenure dates to the fourth century, was imprisoned for two years, threatened with death, and cruelly treated by those who hoped to procure a heretical statement from him. But such a statement was never forthcoming.

Likewise, in the case of the sixth-century pope, Vigilius. Vigilius was a heretic before becoming pope, and his accession to the papacy owed much to the baleful influence of Theodora, wife of the emperor, who expected him to continue in office as a heretic. Nevertheless, once he occupied the chair of St. Peter, his views underwent dramatic change. "Formerly," he wrote, "I spoke wrongly and foolishly. Though unworthy, I am Vicar of Blessed Peter." The reward for Vigilius was ten years of "white" martyrdom ending in a painful and ignominious death.*

---

* See Warren H. Carroll, *The Building of Christendom* (1987), pp. 31-33, 168, 172-78.

Appendix B

Biblical Quotations on
Courtship and Marriage

ON PURITY

"Let us not commit fornication" (St. Paul in *1 Corinthians* 10:8).

"Anyone who so much as looks at a woman with lust has already committed adultery" (Jesus in *Matthew* 5:28).

"Do not let sin reign over your body so that you obey its lusts" (St. Paul in *Romans* 6:12).

"Do not even speak of immorality and uncleanness... Obscenity, foolish talk and scurrility is out of place" in the language of a Christian (St. Paul in *Ephesians* 5:3-4).

"The fruit of the spirit is charity, joy, peace, patience, kindness, goodness, faith, modesty, continency" (St. Paul in *Galatians* 5:22).

"This is the will of God, your sanctification: that you abstain from immorality; that you learn how to possess His vessel in holiness and honor" [God's vessel meaning the body] (St. Paul in *1 Thessalonians* 4:4).

"If thy right eye is an occasion of sin to thee, pluck it out... and if thy right hand is an occasion of sin to thee, cut it off and cast it from thee; for it is better for

thee that one of thy members should be lost than that thy whole body should go into Hell" (Jesus in *Matthew* 5:29-30).

"Immorality, uncleanness, lust, evil desire and covetousness... because of these things the wrath of God comes upon unbelievers" (St. Paul in *Colossians* 3:5-6).

"The lips of an adulteress drip with honey and her mouth is smoother than oil; but in the end she is as bitter as wormwood, as sharp as a two-edged sword. Her feet go down to death" (*Proverbs* 5:3-5).

Of your neighbor's wife: *"Let her not captivate you with her glance!"* (*Proverbs* 6:25).

Advice to men: *"Be not intimate with a strange woman lest you fall into her snares... gaze not about the lanes of a city... avert your glance from an attractive woman; gaze not upon the beauty of another's wife... dine not with a married woman... lest your heart be drawn to her"* (*Sirach* 9:3, 7-9). *"If you have daughters, keep them chaste and do not be indulgent to them... let them not parade their charms before men"* (*Sirach* 7:24 and 42:12).

St. John's *Book of Revelation* (the *Apocalypse*) is not long, consisting of only twenty-two short chapters. Yet it denounces the sin of premarital sex (fornication) no less than nine times and speaks out against adultery, harlotry, and whores six times. This adds up to fifteen separate references to sexual abuse. For additional references, see *Ecclesiastes* 7:26; *Sirach* 26:9-12, 15-18; *Proverbs* 5 (all of it); 6:20-35; 7 (all of it); 22:14; 30:20.

REGARDING A WISE CHOICE OF FRIENDS

We are all sinners, and as such we must be merciful

toward others, just as God is unfailingly kind and compassionate toward us. He is ever ready to forgive, provided we are truly sorry for our offenses and willing to make amends (*Luke* 17:3). Nor are we to judge others (*Matthew* 7:1; *Luke* 6:37). God alone judges.

None of this, however, should be taken to mean that we are to tolerate behavior that is openly sinful. On the contrary, those among us who sin openly and persist in such conduct are to be warned, and if they refuse to heed our warning, they are to be shunned. Christ Himself said as much (*Matthew* 18:15-17), and His meaning is crystal clear from the totality of the gospel message.

To be sure, Christ dined with sinners. But some of them were not so much sinners as social outcasts, like Zacchaeus, while others had repented by the time they made contact with Jesus. The principal points to bear in mind with reference to Jesus' public appearances are:

1. That He dined as a preacher in His preaching capacity. He was not taking a girlfriend to cocktail hours, and
2. There is no evidence that He engaged in small talk.

On the contrary, He is cited as having lectured both host and fellow guests for social lapses (*Luke* chapter 14).

At one dinner party given by a leading Pharisee, Jesus outraged His host by:

1. Working a cure on the Sabbath,
2. Upbraiding the other guests when they maneuvered for high positions at table, and
3. Chiding His host for not inviting a broader cross-section of society.

He even hinted that Jews could not count on automatic admission to the dinner party that counted most. At another banquet, a female penitent bathed His feet with her tears, then wiped them dry with her hair, and anointed them with ointment. When the host complained that Jesus was inadvertently accepting the ministrations of a loose woman, Jesus turned on His accuser and rebuked him for ignoring his duty as host: *"Thou gavest me no water for my feet... Thou gavest me no kiss... Thou didst not anoint my head with oil"* (*Luke* 7:36-49).

For additional Scripture passages dealing with Christian behavior toward those who are openly and persistently sinful, see the following:

1. Christ Himself said that if your brother sins, reprimand him; if this does not suffice, do so in the company of others; and if he still persists, *"Treat him as you would the Gentile or the tax collector"* (i.e., shun him). See *Matthew* 18:15-17; *Titus* 3:10.

2. Christ also said that if a town refuses to receive your message, shake the dust of that town from your feet and move on (*Luke* 10:11-15). He was not one to suffer fools gladly; nor did He recommend the practice to His disciples.

3. St. Paul tells us not to socialize or dine with those who are immoral, foul-mouthed, greedy, or drunkards. *"Expel the wicked man from your midst,"* he adds (*1 Corinthians* 5:9-13), warning that:

4. Evil companionships corrupt good morals (*1 Corinthians* 15:33).

5. *"Men will be lovers of self and money, proud, arrogant... ungrateful... profane, inhuman, implacable, slanderous, and licentious, brutal, hating the good... stay clear of them"* (*2 Timothy* 3:2-5).

6. *"Avoid"* those who *"cause dissensions and*

scandals contrary to the doctrine that you have learned" (*Romans* 16:17).

7. *"Avoid any brother who strays from the straight path"* (*2 Thessalonians* 3:6 and 14).

8. *"Warn the heretic once, then a second time. After that have nothing to do with him. You must view such a person as perverted and sinful"* (*Titus* 3:10).

9. Paul twice advises his flock to "let a curse" be upon any preacher who departs from the approved, orthodox line of teaching (*Galatians* 1:9).

10. John the Evangelist speaks in similar terms: *"If anyone comes to you and does not bring this doctrine* [i.e., proves to be a heretic], *do not receive him, for he who welcomes him is a sharer in his evil works"* (*2 John* 1:10-11).

11. Old Testament quotations: *"He who touches pitch blackens his hand; he who associates with an impious man learns his ways"* (*Sirach* 13:1). See also *Sirach* 12:1-7; 22:12-13; *Psalm* 14 (15):4 *("Despise the reprobate, honor those who fear the Lord");* also *Psalm* 138 (139):21-22.

12. St. Anthony of the desert warned fellow Christians of Alexandria to "have no fellowship with the most impious Arians, for there is no communication between light and darkness...creation itself is angry with them" (Warren Carroll, *The Building of Christendom,* p. 21).

ON THE PERMANENCE OF MARRIAGE (INDISSOLUBILITY)

Please note—the quotations that follow are the only

ones to be found in the New Testament on the subject
of divorce:

*"Everyone who puts away his wife and marries another
commits adultery; and he who marries a woman who has
been put away from her husband commits adultery"*
(Jesus in *Luke* 16:18).

*"A man shall leave his father and mother and cleave
to his wife, and the two shall become one flesh...what
therefore God has joined together let no man put asunder...Whoever puts away his wife and marries another
commits adultery against her; and if the wife puts away
her husband and marries another, she commits adultery"*
(Jesus in *Mark* 10:7-12).

*"Everyone who puts away his wife, save on account
of immorality, causes her to commit adultery; and he who
marries a woman who has been put away commits adultery"* (Jesus in *Matthew* 5:32). Note that Jesus speaks of
a man putting his wife away (i.e., separation on account
of immorality). He does not speak of a man's right to
remarry. See also *Matthew* 19:3-9.

*"Not I, but the Lord commands that a wife is not to
depart from her husband, and if she departs, that she is
to remain unmarried or be reconciled to her husband.
And let not a husband put away his wife"* (St. Paul in
1 Corinthians 7:10-11).

ON THE RELATIONSHIP BETWEEN HUSBANDS AND WIVES

*"Wives be submissive to your husbands...husbands
love your wives"* (St. Paul in *Ephesians* 5:22; *Colossians*
3:18; *1 Corinthians* 11:3 and 9; also St. Peter in *1 Peter*
3:1-7).

Husbands are to love their wives as they love "their own bodies" and as Christ loves His Church (St. Paul in *Ephesians* 5:25, 28, 33; and St. Peter in *1 Peter* 3:7).

In the Garden of Eden, God said, *"It is not good that the man be alone; I will make him a helpmate"* (*Genesis* 2:18). See also *Genesis* 3:16 referring to husbandly "dominion" over the wife.

Appendix C

More on Marriage

IMPEDIMENTS TO MARRIAGE

Impediments to marriage which, according to present Church law, could render a marriage null and void in the eyes of the Church and thus constitute grounds for annulment include insufficient age, use of force, closeness of blood relationship, pre-existing marriage, and a vow of virginity that is public and perpetual. There are several others as well.

THE PAULINE PRIVILEGE

On the basis of one of the passages in St. Paul's writings (*1 Corinthians* 7:12-15), the Church reserves the right to dissolve a non-sacramental marriage between two unbaptized persons in accord with certain conditions: (a) there has been a sincere conversion to the Catholic faith by one of the parties, (b) the second party harasses the first in the practice of his or her faith to the point where it provokes grave sin, and (c) reconciliation appears impossible (see Canon Law, c. 1143-1150). One should perhaps note, in addition, that the Pauline Privilege has been a bit tenuous over the years since there is a certain hesitancy in Christian Tradition about interpreting St. Paul's words to allow for more than separation, which is all that is explicitly granted. See *Jerome Biblical Commentary* (1968), p. 264.

MOTHER TERESA TO ENGAGED COUPLES

"You are the future of family life. You are the future of the joy of loving. You are the future of making your life something beautiful for God...a pure love. That you love a girl or that you love a boy is beautiful, but don't spoil it, don't destroy it. Keep it pure. Keep your heart virgin. Keep your love virgin so that on the day of your marriage you can give something beautiful to each other...the joy of a pure love."

ST. JEANNE-FRANÇOISE DE CHANTAL AND POPE JOHN PAUL II ON CHASTITY AND CHILD-BEARING

St. Jeanne-Françoise de Chantal (1572-1641), widowed mother of five, had a married daughter who was tempted to limit her family to four children because she craved the social whirl, dreaded the thought of baby after baby, and was concerned that she wouldn't be able to provide for additional children "according to their station in life." Saint Jeanne advised her daughter as follows:

> My dearest child, you are too fond of the things of earth. What do you fear? That the number of your children deprive you of the means of educating and settling them in life according to their birth? Apprehend nothing of the kind, I beg you, for that would be wronging the wise providence of Him who gives them to you, and Who is sufficiently good and rich to support them, to provide for them as will be expedient for His honor and their salvation. This is all that we should desire for our children, and not aggrandizement in this miserable and fleeting world.
> Courage, then, my very dear daughter!

Receive with love and from the hand of God all the little creatures that He gives you. Take very great care of them. Cherish them tenderly, and rear them entirely in the fear of God, and not in vanity (Wendy Leifeld, *Mothers of the Saints* (1991), 149-50, quoting Monsignor Bongaud's biography of Chantal).

Pope John Paul II addressing participants of a Family Ministry Conference on 28 April 1990, declared that:

If the family is established on a healthy basis, it will find the way to accept children generously as a concrete sign of its love of life and as a clear witness of its trust in divine Providence, which never abandons those who entrust themselves to it with active serenity. This goes especially for young families who, if they are trained in a Christian spirit, will not let themselves be conquered by an unjustified fear of having children, and will find a way to overcome the many groundless and selfish tendencies toward putting off giving birth.

To members of the student group, Univ, at about the same time, the Holy Father said,

Tell your boyfriends and girlfriends that they should be proud to live Christian purity, that they should love the wonderful gift of virginity, that they should appreciate increasingly the value of temperance and detachment in a world wedded to consumerism (reported in *The Wanderer,* 24 May 1990).

DAILY PRAYER FOR A MARRIED COUPLE

Thank you, Lord, for the graces which today You planted deep in our souls through the Sacrament of Matrimony. May these sources of strength and devotion remain always and grow like the mustard seed. Help us to love You by loving each other; to understand the meaning of life by understanding each other; to draw closer to You by our closer union; and to use the joys and sorrows of our life together as a means of gaining ever more faith, hope, and charity. O God, You have helped us come together; help us to stay together. With Your help we have resolved our differences through ever deeper love and mutual understanding and used each occasion to forge greater unity; with Your help we will continue to turn weakness into strength! May our marriage be fruitful as we labor in the great vineyard of this world; and may we come to our eternal rest through each other, with each other, and in each other. Amen.

Appendix D

Holy Communion

ON THE EUCHARIST

Apart from Church Tradition, there are several key passages in Scripture which support the Catholic belief in Christ's real presence. See *Matthew* 26:26-28; *Luke* 22:19-20; and *Mark* 14:22-27. See also the passage in which Jesus explains what He means to His scandalized followers: *John* 6:1-13, 48-67. St. Paul speaks of receiving the "Body of Christ" worthily (*1 Corinthians* 10:16 and 11:24-29). We also have the testimony of St. Ignatius of Antioch (107 A.D.): "The Eucharist is the Flesh of our Savior Jesus Christ." Likewise, St. Justin, writing in 145 A.D.: "The Eucharist...is both the Flesh and the Blood of Jesus."

ON DAILY COMMUNION

Pope Pius X (1903-14) was the first pontiff to recommend this practice for all the faithful, barring serious inconvenience. For his text, he chose the words of the "Our Father": "Give us this day our daily bread."

PROPER DRESS FOR CHURCH

The wearing of one's "Sunday best" is as natural as it is becoming to those who join in divine worship. The Lord went to great lengths in the Old Testament to specify that Church appointments, furnishings, and decorations should be made of the very finest materials (such as gold, precious gems, and rare woods). See *Exodus,* chapters 25-28; *Psalm* 28 (29):2; and *Psalm* 95 (96):9 *("Worship the Lord in holy attire")*. Clearly, He wanted a certain atmosphere.

Appendix E

Penance or the Sacrament of Reconciliation

SCRIPTURAL BASIS

Christ forgave sins (*Luke* 5:18-24) and passed this power on to Peter, who was to act as His representative: *"Whatever you shall bind on earth shall be bound in Heaven, and whatever you shall loose on earth shall be loosed in Heaven"* (*Matt.* 16:13-19). Jesus also gave the power of absolution to the apostles as a whole: *"Whose sins you shall forgive, they shall be forgiven, and whose sins you shall retain, they shall be retained"* (*John* 20:23). We also have the testimony of two saints, James and John: *"Confess your sins to one another"* (*James* 5:16; *1 John* 1:8-9).

WHAT IS SIN?

Very simply, sin is an offense against God. Sins may be minor (venial) or major (mortal). While we are *obliged* to confess all mortal sins, we are urged to do the same with venial sins insofar as we are aware of them. Three conditions must obtain for a sin to be mortal:

1. The offense must be serious,
2. We must be fully aware of its gravity, and
3. There must be full consent of the will.

If any one of these conditions is missing, the sin in question is venial.

EXAMPLES OF SERIOUS SIN

Mortal sins would include serious offenses against the Ten Commandments or any of the seven capital sins:

Ten Commandments:
1. I, the Lord, am your God. You shall not have false gods before me (such as money, sex, or worldly success);
2. Thou shalt not take the name of the Lord your God in vain (no swearing);
3. Keep holy the Sabbath (by attending Mass on Sunday or late Saturday and trying as much as possible to avoid working on Sunday);
4. Honor thy father and thy mother;
5. Thou shalt not kill (another human being except in self-defense or just punishment);
6. Thou shalt not commit adultery;
7. Thou shalt not steal;
8. Thou shalt not bear false witness against thy neighbor;
9. Thou shalt not covet thy neighbor's wife;
10. Thou shalt not covet thy neighbor's goods.

The Seven Capital Sins:
1. Pride,
2. Covetousness,
3. Lust,
4. Anger,
5. Gluttony,
6. Envy,
7. Sloth.

EXAMINATION OF CONSCIENCE

It is often helpful to think in terms of what we might

have done to please God but didn't. In other words, we should confess not only the things we *did* to offend God, but also things we *did not* do that might have been done had we been more considerate or less preoccupied with self.

WHAT ONE SAYS TO THE PRIEST IN CONFESSION

To begin: "Bless me father, for I have sinned. It is three weeks (or whatever period) since my last confession. Since that time, I have..." (list the sins you have committed and for each one the approximate number of times).

To conclude (after the priest gives you your penance), say the Act of Contrition: "O my God, I am heartily sorry for having offended Thee, and I detest all my sins because I dread the loss of Heaven and the pains of Hell. But most of all because I offend Thee, Who art all good and deserving of all my love. I firmly resolve, with the help of Thy grace, to confess my sins, to do penance, and to amend my life. Amen."

TO RECEIVE COMMUNION

St. Paul warns that he who consumes the host or drinks the cup of the Lord unworthily *"will be guilty of the body and blood of the Lord"* (*1 Corinthians* 11:27). In order to receive the Eucharist worthily, we must confess all mortal sins committed since our last confession. Naturally, we will feel closer to God, and, therefore, make a better approach to Communion, if we confess on a regular basis such as once every three weeks. In the unlikely event that there is nothing to confess, one may mention the sins of one's past life and express remorse for them even though they have already been confessed and forgiven. This can be a good practice.

OPPORTUNITIES FOR MASS AND CONFESSION

There can be little excuse for not receiving the Sacraments regularly. The Church goes out of its way to make them available, particularly in large cities. Take, for example, New York, where St. Jean's Church (Lexington and 76th Street) has daily Mass at 6:15, 7, 7:30, 8, 9, 12:10, 1, 5:30 and 7:30, while confessions are heard every day from 11:40 to 12:10, 4 to 5:30, and 7 to 7:30. St. Agnes Church (between Lexington and Third Avenue at 43rd Street) offers Masses every half hour from 7 to 9 A.M. as well as at mid-day and during the late afternoon. Confessions are heard at all of the same times. What an extraordinary opportunity, and one more reason to be a Catholic! Check the schedule of churches nearest you.

Appendix F

Bearing Witness

St. Peter wrote: *"Be ready always with an answer for everyone who asks a reason for the hope that is in you"* (*1 Peter* 3:15). Jesus told His disciples, and He was speaking to us as well:

> *Do not let them intimidate you...What I tell you in darkness, speak in the light. What you hear in private proclaim from the housetops...Whoever acknowledges me before men I will acknowledge before my Father in Heaven. Whoever disowns me before men I will disown before my Father in Heaven (Matthew 10:26-33).*

The Second Vatican Council declared that:

> The laity must be specially formed [on the subject of religion] to engage in conversation with others...A true apostle looks for opportunities to announce Christ by words addressed either to non-believers with a view to leading them to faith or to believers with a view to instructing and strengthening them (See the Council's *Decree on the Apostolate of the Laity*, sections 6 and 31).

Appendix G

Heaven and Hell in the Bible

HEAVEN

"Eye has not seen, nor ear heard, nor has it so much as dawned on man what God has prepared for those who love Him" (St. Paul in *1 Corinthians* 2:9). Jesus spoke of Heaven as "Paradise" (*Luke* 23:43). He also said that each child has its own angel in Heaven (*Matthew* 18:10). Hence the beautiful children's prayer: "Angel of God, my guardian dear, to whom God's love commits me here, ever this day be at my side, to light and guard, to rule and guide."

HEAVEN COMPARED WITH HELL

Jesus said, *"The just will shine like the sun, while evil-doers shall be hurled into the fiery furnace to wail and grind their teeth"* (*Matthew* 13:40-43). He also referred to Heaven as eternal life and to Hell as eternal punishment (*Matthew* 25:41-46).

HELL

Jesus described the fire of Hell as "unquenchable" and "everlasting" (*Matthew* 3:12 and 25:41); spoke of Hell in terms of darkness (*Matthew* 8:12); said that good and evil would be separated on the day of judgment as a farmer separates wheat from the chaff (*Matthew* 13:30); and stressed that the gate to eternal life was narrow and the road difficult with "few" entering, whereas the gate to Hell was wide and the road easy (with "many" going that way). See *Matthew* 7:13-14. On one occasion, He told the Pharisees that they were a "brood of vipers" bound for Hell: *"How,"* He queried, *"can you escape condemnation to Gehenna?"* (Jerusalem's smoldering garbage dump). See *Matthew* 5:22; 23:33.

On another occasion, Jesus said that on the day of judgment we would be held accountable not only for deliberate sin, but for every idle word we utter (*Matthew* 12:36); hence the concept of venial sin. Jesus let it be known that an entire town, Capharnaum, would be condemned to Hell for its iniquitous behavior (*Matthew* 11:20-24). And once, after Our Lord cured a paralytic, He cautioned him, *"Sin no more lest something worse befall you!"* (*John* 5:1-15). See also *Luke* 16:19-26 for the parable about Lazarus and the rich man and Christ's reference to a "fixed abyss" between Heaven and Hell.

Appendix H

Scriptural Basis for the Other Sacraments

Anointing of the Sick
(Formerly known as Extreme Unction)

James 5:14-16: *"Is there anyone sick among you? He should ask for the priests of the Church. They in turn are to pray over him, anointing him with oil in the name of the Lord. This prayer uttered in Faith will reclaim the one who is ill, and the Lord will restore him to health. If he has committed any sins, forgiveness will be his."* See also *Mark* 6:13: *"They expelled many demons, anointed the sick with oil, and worked many cures."*

Baptism

Jesus said: *"Go forth and make disciples of all nations, baptizing them in the name of the Father and of the Son and of the Holy Spirit"* (*Matthew* 28:19-20). He also told Nicodemus, *"I solemnly assure you, no one can enter into God's kingdom without being begotten of water and the Holy Spirit"* (*John* 3:5). Jesus Himself was, of course, baptized by John in the River Jordan.

Confirmation

See *Acts* 8:14-17 and other passages similar to it. On being a "soldier of Christ," see *Ephesians* 6:13-17.

Appendix I

More on the Myth of Overpopulation

Anyone seriously interested in the question of population should read such respected economists as Julian Simon, author of *Population Matters,* and Jacqueline Kasun, author of *The War Against Population: The Economics and Ideology of Population Control.*

Contrary to what one would gather from the media, air pollution and other environmental hazards have become less, rather than more, severe in certain areas. Los Angeles, for example, has made notable advances in improving the quality of its air, especially in the 30 years since it came to be known as "Smog City."

The world's supply of natural resources, again contrary to expectation, has more than kept pace with rising birthrates. Interestingly enough, the price of many vital commodities such as oil, electricity, and natural gas has actually declined over the years. Copper, nickel, chrome, tin, and tungsten are all cheaper than they once were, giving the lie to one of Ehrlich's better known theories. At the same time, many of yesterday's so-called "essential" resources such as whale oil and coal are no longer essential thanks to a variety of technological breakthroughs. Natural gas alone is estimated to be in large enough supply to last 1,000 to 2,500 years. When it comes to food, the outlook is again encouraging. A good many developing countries (33, according to the *New York Times*) have realized more than enough gains in agricultural productivity to sustain a burgeoning populace. During the period 1970 to 1985, the percentage of people living in poverty in developing countries fell from 52 percent to 44 percent. Meanwhile, here at home, the United States labor force is expected to remain steady over the next 35 years.*

On the personal level, if Catholic leaders have been more insistent than most about bringing additional food to the table in lieu of turning people away, they are not alone. In countries such as Egypt and Iran, religious values similar to our own have acted as a formidable barrier to the introduction of artificial birth control. Faithful Muslims and devout Hindus believe that every child is a gift from God. The celebrated Indian nationalist, Mahatma Gandhi, preached that marital union without the desire for progeny was a crime.

Scientific research, funded in large part by the Ford and Rockefeller Foundations, has led to the discovery of greatly superior strains of wheat and rice which have revolutionized food production around the world. Before the utilization of new grains such as the IR-S in places like Vietnam, many nations were hard put to meet their domestic needs. Today, these same countries find themselves in the export business. Improvements in well-digging, fertilizers, and the use of polyethylene ditch liners played a major role in India's "Green Revolution" which has caused land values in certain areas to soar as much as 600 percent in the space of a few years. Here, as elsewhere, the migration of rural people to urban areas was completely reversed.

The United States, which produces more food than it can consume (during the Great Depression of 1929 to 1941, American farmers were paid to plow food under),

---

* See *New York Times,* 30 April 1992, p. A12; Robert J. Hutchinson, "Overpopulation: The Myth That Won't Die," *Catholic Twin Circle,* 13 January 1991, pp. 10-11; also Barbara Insel's excellent article, "A World Awash in Grain," *Foreign Affairs* (Spring 1985).

has long taken upon itself the task of relieving overseas famine, and there is no limit to what can be accomplished provided there is sufficient capital. The point is that one must never underestimate the power of human ingenuity when it comes to devising systems capable of sustaining life under the most adverse conditions. Synthetic foods, ocean floor farming, solar energy, and the coming revolution in transport will act to counterbalance whatever pressure may be generated by a rising birthrate.

When all is said and done, Planned Parenthood will go on sponsoring plans for the prevention of parenthood, all in the name of prudence and charity, and it will do so in spite of the fact that the myth of overpopulation is just that, a myth, in spite of the fact that there is no reliable evidence to show that the world is headed for catastrophe, and in spite of the fact that there is no demonstrable link between secular-materialist policies aimed at guaranteeing high standards of living and that most elusive of all human conditions—happiness. We must therefore be on constant guard against fraudulent claims and false alarms.

Appendix J

Famous Orphans and Children from Large Families

The following individuals were born into families of:

7 children: George Washington, greatest of all American leaders (he also lost his father at age 11); St. Thomas Aquinas, greatest of all Church thinkers and writers, a real genius.

8 children: Charles Dickens (the family was also very poor).

9 children: Grover Cleveland, one of the better two-term American presidents (his father died when he was 16).

10 children: Thomas Jefferson, James Madison, and James Polk (all three presidents of the United States). Also Daniel Webster (9th of 10 children) and John C. Calhoun, two of the all-time great senators.

11 children: Washington Irving, one of the greatest of early American writers (while his older brothers went to college, he went to work); also St. Rose of Lima. Both Rose and Irving were the **last** of 11!

12 children: Harriet Beecher Stowe, author of *Uncle Tom's Cabin,* and Franz Schubert, famous musical composer who wrote the beautiful "Ave Maria" and other sublime works; also Matt Talbot, "patron saint" of Alcoholics Anonymous.

13 children: St. Ignatius Loyola, founder of the Jesuits, was the last of 13; also Frances Cabrini, first American saint.

15 children: John Marshall, greatest of all chief justices of the United States Supreme Court.

16 children: Henry Clay, one of the greatest of early American statesmen (he lost his father at the age of 4).

17 children: Benjamin Franklin, most extraordinary of American "renaissance men," was a scientific savant, writer, diplomat, wit, and practically everything else one can think of.

21 children: Enrico Caruso, perhaps the greatest tenor who ever lived, was born 18th in a family of 21 children.

25 children: St. Catherine of Siena, 24th of 25 children, was called the greatest woman in Christendom, although she lived to be only 33.

Among the men and women who lost one or both parents at an early age, in addition to Washington and Cleveland, one can mention: Jefferson (at the age of 14), Franklin (ran away from home), Alexander Hamilton (11), Calhoun (14), Jackson, Clay, Lincoln, and Robert E. Lee—when Lee was 5, his father wandered away from home, never to return. Also Theodore Roosevelt (19), Franklin Roosevelt (a freshman in college), Herbert Hoover (lost both of his parents by the age of 8), Mark Twain (11), Andrew Carnegie (19), Saint John Bosco (lost his father when he was only two and his mother never remarried).

In sports, one can name Jackie Robinson, Babe Ruth, and Joe Louis. Foreigners whose names come to mind would include Alexander Solzhenitsyn (lost his father before he was even born), Churchill (20), Stalin (11), Hitler (13)—not all achievers were morally good!—

Chiang Kai-shek (9), Confucius (an orphan), Genghis Khan (9).

In the ranks of famous women, one thinks of Maria Camacho, the Mexican martyr who died in 1935 defending her Church and shouting, "Viva Cristo Rey" (Long Live Christ the King!). Shot at the age of 28, she was no stranger to suffering. Her mother had died when she was a few months old, and subsequently she lived with her grandmother and father, then with her father and stepmother, then again with her father and grandmother.

Blessed Edith Stein, martyred in the Dutch holocaust, was the youngest of seven when she lost her father at the age of two. St. Thérèse of Lisieux, one of nine children, lost her mother when she was only a toddler, and her father never remarried. Blessed Kateri Tekakwitha lost her mother at the age of four and she was raised by fiercely anti-Christian relatives. St. Elizabeth Bayley Seton, the first native-born American to be canonized, lost her mother when she was only three.

Appendix K

Some Useful Organizations, Addresses, and Phone Numbers

1. Engaged Encounter: Consult your local priest or bishop if there is no listing in the local telephone directory.

2. Marriage Encounter (to make good marriages better): Consult your local priest or bishop if there is no listing in the local telephone directory.

3. Retrouvaille (for couples experiencing grave difficulties):
   National Headquarters:
      Tel. 713-455-2027
      (formerly 817-284-7078)
   Michigan location:
      495 East 14 Mile Road
      Clawson, Michigan 48107
      Tel. 313-585-5544

4. The Couple to Couple League (for couples who wish to learn more about Natural Family Planning and related topics from other couples):
   Box 111184
   Cincinnati, Ohio 45211
   Tel. 513-661-7612

5. Seton Home Study (one of a number of excellent home school programs):
   Mrs. Mary Kay Clark
   1350 Progress Drive
   P.O. Box 396
   Front Royal, VA 22630

Part 7

Questionnaire for Engaged Couples

What follows is a list of questions aimed at helping engaged parties come to a better understanding of one another. By exploring areas of disagreement, as well as agreement, it is hoped that their marriage, when it occurs, will be that much more secure:

1. Are both of you open to the possibility of having children, and do you know that without such openness you cannot be validly married in the Church?

2. Are you agreed on the extent to which you might wish to be involved in Church-related activities (social, financial, religious, etc.)?

3. Are you agreed on the roles and duties you envision for one another in marriage? Who, in other words, will do what?

4. Are you agreed on basic goals—for instance, the importance you will attach to social status, money, and possessions?

5. Do you feel generally relaxed in the presence of your future spouse? If not, have you been able to identify the source of the anxiety or fear?

6. Are you agreed on how to handle finances—budgeting, checking accounts, credit cards, etc.?

7. Have you discussed how you feel about the celebration of holidays and other special occasions?

8. Are both of you good listeners? If not, have you discussed what you are going to do to improve communication since it is vital for a sound marriage?

9. Do you think you are seeing enough of each other and engaging in enough serious conversation to grow in sensitivity, depth of appreciation, and communication skills? Are you aware that there will be an ongoing need for such time together once you are married? How and when you do plan to make "quality time" available to one another?

10. Are you aware of any personal shortcomings in your partner? Do you understand that they could undermine your chance for a happy marriage? And have you warned your spouse-to-be of what to expect from you along this line?

11. Are you agreed on the kind of wedding you want, how much you wish to spend, and where the money will come from? The burden should not be such that it works a severe strain on either side of the family.

12. Are you prepared to put your eyes, ears, and heart under strict lock and key as a safeguard to marital fidelity, and are you aware that this will entail a measure of self-sacrifice?

13. Have you discussed how you would react to changes in fortune (social status and/or career) that might occur suddenly and unexpectedly?

14. Are you prepared to accept each other as you are, or do you expect your partner to change? Unless you are content with the status quo, you could be headed for difficulties. If something about your partner irritates you, chances are it will be twice as irritating after the wedding. Those who are conscientious will try hard to please their spouse, but change along this line can be difficult, if not impossible, even with the best of intentions.

15. If your spouse seems pointed in the direction of heavy drinking, gambling, or sexual promiscuity, are you prepared to live with the consequences? Catholic marriage requires nothing less than total commitment under any and all circumstances.

16. Are you agreed on the amount of time you would regard as acceptable for the other person to be away with "the boys" or "the girls," with relatives, or on a religious retreat once you are married?

17. Do you share the same views on child-rearing when it comes to discipline, education, and spiritual formation?

18. Are you prepared to accept the fact that your spouse, far from being able to relieve all of your personal problems, hangups, and frustrations, may actually add to the burden?

19. Are you aware, as a Catholic contemplating marriage, that your loyalty and determination to go the distance must be such that they will sustain you through any eventuality including severe illness, paralysis, childlessness, insanity, infidelity, or whatever else may befall you? Do you realize that mar-

riage could prove to be extremely difficult in certain instances and that such difficulty is rarely foreseen?

20. Are you clear on why the Church condemns abortion and artificial contraception? Are you aware, in addition, that Natural Family Planning is permissible only if there are "grave" reasons for using it?

21. If you are marrying a non-Catholic, are you clear on your responsibility to educate all children in the knowledge and practice of your faith? Is the non-Catholic willing to cooperate along this line? And are you aware that anything less than full cooperation could make your task a painful one?

22. If you have been living together with your spouse-to-be, are you aware that this is a serious offense in the eyes of Christ and His Church, that you should go to confession, call a halt to sexual intercourse, establish separate residences, and do whatever penance is prescribed by the priest?

23. Have you discussed your concept of the role of a "working" mother, as compared with that of the traditional "homemaker," along with the role to be played by the "working" mother's husband?

24. If your spouse-to-be plans to work full-time outside the home, are you prepared to bear the full burden of cooking, cleaning, and child care? If not, what kind of division of labor do you envision?

25. Are you agreed on your priorities regarding child-rearing, community service, work, and personal fulfillment?

26. How do you plan to settle disagreements? Who will be the final arbiter in disputes affecting the well-being of the family after all avenues of compromise are exhausted?

27. Are you prepared to deal with the kind of pressure that may be generated by in-laws? And have you discussed ways of guarding your relationship should it be threatened by such pressure?

28. Do you agree that a loving relationship between you and your spouse should be your first aim in marriage, second only to your relationship with God, and that it should take precedence over the demands of in-laws, friends, associates, career, and even children, since their ultimate welfare depends on the strength and durability of the marriage?

29. Are you clear on the Church's basic teachings? If not, are you prepared to do what is necessary to become better acquainted? Beyond this, are you prepared to share your convictions and religious views with others, a responsibility underscored by Vatican Council II?

30. If you plan to travel together before marriage without sharing the same bed, are you aware that such proximity, especially if it involves long distances over extended periods, is likely to be an occasion of sin and that it may also give scandal? Do you realize that you have an obligation to care about what other people think and that it is up to you to avoid any course of action that could lead others to sin? You yourself may not be doing anything intrinsically wrong, but, as St. Paul reminds us, there is such a thing as sinning against others by wounding their *"weak conscience,"* and when you do this, *"you sin against*

Christ" (*1 Corinthians* 8:7-13). We are not even permitted to do what is perfectly legitimate if, in so doing, others will be *"scandalized or morally weakened"* (*Romans* 14:21). As Christ Himself put it, *"Things that cause sin will inevitably occur, but woe to the person through whom they occur. It would be better for him if a millstone were put around his neck and he be thrown into the sea"* (*Luke* 17:1-2).

31. Is your relationship based a great deal on feeling, such as physical attraction and romantic excitement, and comparatively little on shared values and goals? If so, you are almost certainly dating the wrong person.

Index

125

SOME ADDITIONAL TITLES

UNIT 6-GEORGE-90, SIGNAL 44 (OH GOD, PLEASE TELL ME WHERE YOU ARE)
by Laurie Balbach-Taylor

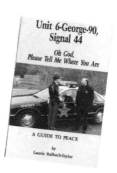

Some careers are more prone to stress than others, but basic problems and their solutions are found in *every* lifestyle. This book is for anyone who wants to find peace. It is a blueprint for seeking and finding God's touch in our lives.

86 pages **$4.50**

THREE STEPS TO SANCTITY
by Fr. Albert J. Shamon

"Nothing in life is worth so much as our becoming saints." A powerful but simple little book on sanctity.

45 pages **$1.00**

OUR LADY SAYS: LOVE PEOPLE
by Fr. Albert J. Shamon

"There are in the end three things that last: faith, hope and love, and the greatest of these is LOVE." A beautiful guide for those seeking insight into the meaning of Christian love.

80 pages **$2.00**

THE GOLD BOOK OF PRAYERS

Small book of prayers, both contemporary and traditional. Scriptural Rosary, Jesus Rosary, and Seven Sorrows Chaplet. Many beautiful prayers and litanies. Ideal for prayer groups.

96 pages **$3.00**

Book Dealers and Distributors:
Faith Publishing Company
P.O. Box 237
Milford, Ohio 45150
1-800-576-6477

Individuals Should Contact:
The Riehle Foundation
P.O. Box 7
Milford, Ohio 45150
513-576-0032

Faith Publishing Company

Faith Publishing Company has been organized as a service for the publishing and distribution of materials that reflect Christian values, and in particular, the teachings of the Catholic Church.

It is dedicated to publication of only those materials that reflect such values.

Faith Publishing Company also publishes books for The Riehle Foundation. The Foundation is a non-profit, tax-exempt producer and distributor of Catholic books and materials worldwide and also supplies hospital and prison ministries, churches, and mission organizations.

For more information on the publications of Faith Publishing Company, contact:

Faith Publishing Company

P.O. BOX 237
MILFORD, OHIO 45150